VOL. 1

INTRODUCTION TO
ANATOMY & PHYSIOLOGY

The Musculoskeletal System

wonders of the
HUMAN
BODY

Dr. Tommy Mitchell

First printing: May 2015

Master Books® is a division of the
New Leaf Publishing Group, Inc.

ISBN: 978-0-89051-865-6
Library of Congress Number: 2015930890

Cover by Diana Bogardus
Interior by Jennifer Bauer

Unless otherwise noted, Scripture quotations are from the
New King James Version of the Bible.

Please consider requesting that a copy of this volume be
purchased by your local library system.

Printed in China

Please visit our website for other great titles:
www.masterbooks.net

For information regarding author interviews, please
contact the publicity department at (870) 438-5288.

Master
Books®
A Division of New Leaf Publishing Group
www.masterbooks.net

Dedication
For my beloved wife, Elizabeth

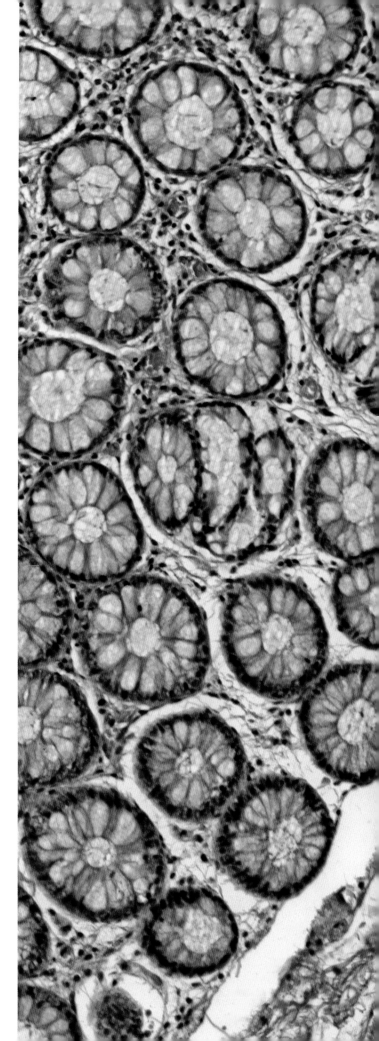

Cross section of glandular ducts

TABLE OF CONTENTS

SECTION 1

FOUNDATIONS

This book is introductory to the anatomy and physiology series, so you've come to the perfect starting off place! You'll be learning about cells, the basic building blocks of the body; tissues, a group of cells that perform similar or related functions; organs, which are tissues that function together; and homeostasis, which is the balance found among all your body functions. God created us and so He knows best how to care for us through all He has made!

"Where were you when I laid the foundations of the earth?" God asked this questions of Job (38:4), referring to the creation of the world. A foundation is the starting place for building something, and a good foundation is needed to create something that will last. Just as God created the heavens and the earth, He created us as well, and knows us more deeply and intricately than science will ever be able to grasp.

For You formed my inward parts; You covered me in my mother's womb. I will praise You, for I am fearfully and wonderfully made; Marvelous are Your works, And that my soul knows very well. My frame was not hidden from You, When I was made in secret, And skillfully wrought in the lowest parts of the earth. Your eyes saw my substance, being yet unformed. And in Your book they all were written, The days fashioned for me, When as yet there were none of them (Psalm 139:13–16).

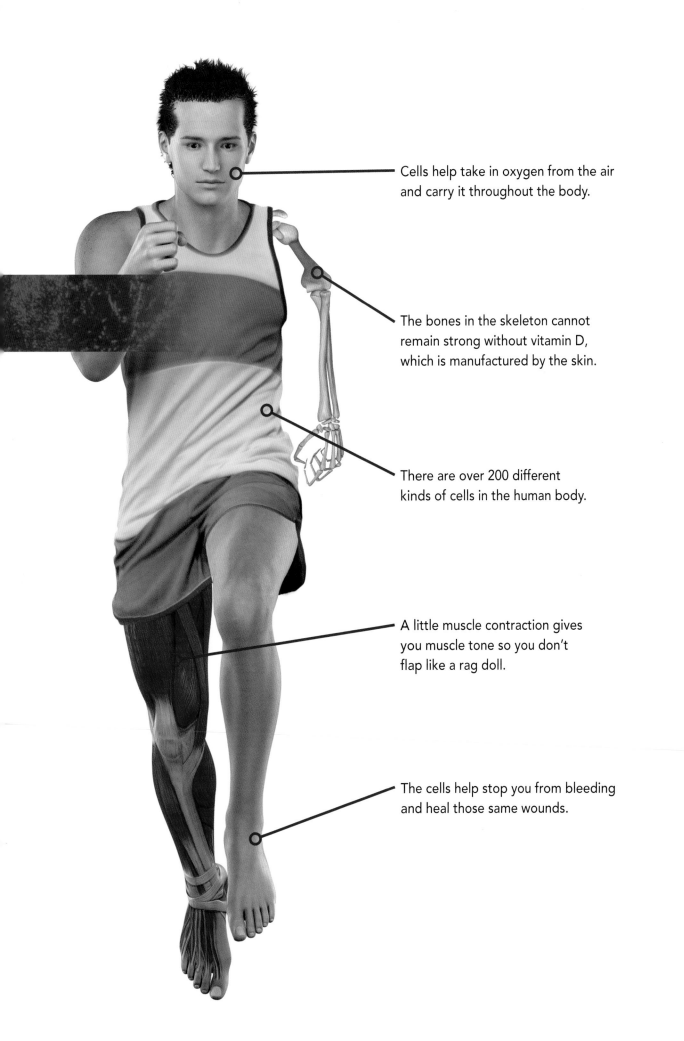

Cells help take in oxygen from the air and carry it throughout the body.

The bones in the skeleton cannot remain strong without vitamin D, which is manufactured by the skin.

There are over 200 different kinds of cells in the human body.

A little muscle contraction gives you muscle tone so you don't flap like a rag doll.

The cells help stop you from bleeding and heal those same wounds.

1

INTRODUCTION

The human body — two arms and two legs, a head, chest, and tummy — seems simple on the surface. In reality, however, it is an incredibly designed orchestra of parts perfectly created to work together. Your body's parts — from the largest bones and organs to the smallest molecules and cells — are put together with a precision no engineer could design. Your body is able to do a remarkable array of things. And it must do many of them nonstop without your attention. This series of books will take you on a guided tour of your own body, giving you a peek into its secrets, large and small, and showing you how it works and how all its parts are designed to work together. Think of this as an owner's manual to the first birthday gift you ever received — the body with which you were born.

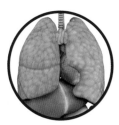

Respiratory System

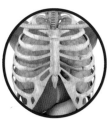

Skeletal System

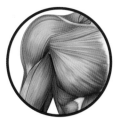

Muscular System

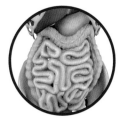

Digestive System

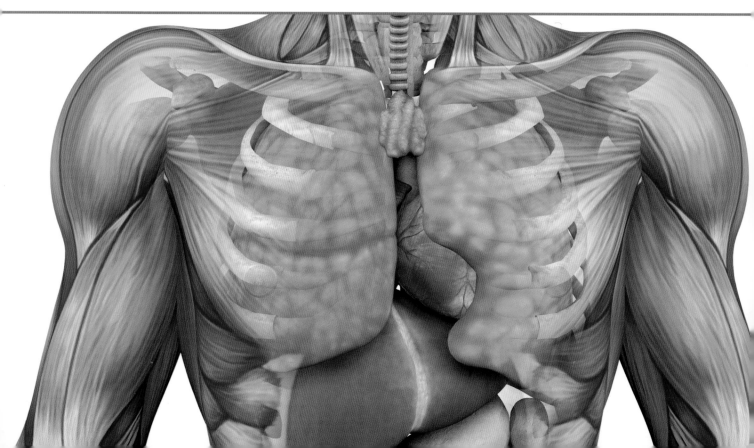

The same body that can use a hammer to drive a nail can hold a feather without crushing it. The same eyes can take in the expanse of the Grand Canyon yet detect faint light from stars many light years away. Your lungs enable you to talk and sing without forgetting to take in oxygen and release carbon dioxide. If you had to think about breathing, you could never go to sleep, for you would die within minutes.

Your digestive system breaks down food into the chemicals you need for energy. Your heart pumps blood through miles of blood vessels to deliver oxygen and nutrients to the most unseen places. Directed by your brain, you walk, run, throw a ball, play a video game, read a book, paint a picture, or even play an instrument. However, the same brain also controls many essential activities inside your body that you are probably not aware of.

What Is Evolution?

In the Bible we read, "In the beginning God created the heavens and the earth" (Genesis 1:1). This theme is repeated time and time again. God is called Creator. In John 1:2 it states, "All things were made through him."

However, there are many people, Christians and non-Christians alike, who do not acknowledge Him as the One who created all things. Instead, they believe in something called evolution.

Rather than accepting God as Creator, they believe that billions of years ago, matter just appeared out of nowhere. Then, they believe, there was a rapid expansion of the universe called the big bang. As this process progressed, the stars and galaxies formed themselves. Then about five billion years ago, our sun was formed and later all the planets in our solar system.

They believe our planet was at first a hot molten blob that eventually cooled and became covered with water. Then all the substances necessary for living things appeared. The first simple life form then sprang into existence by accident.

Then over the next few billion years, living things became more and more complex until at last man appeared on the scene. In this view, man is no more than a cosmic accident, the result of chemicals bumping together over millions of years. Basically, we are then just a highly evolved animal. What folly is a belief such as this!

As we go through our study of the human body, you will see how absurd it is to think that these marvelously complex systems assembled themselves by accident. We are not an accident. We are made in the image of our wonderful Creator God. God tells us in the Bible where we came from: "Then God said, 'Let Us make man in Our image, according to Our likeness' " (Genesis 1:26).

Your bones give your body shape and support even while they grow, your skin protects you from the outside world, your blood carries oxygen and the tiny tools to fight off harmful germs, your liver manufactures chemicals you need while it breaks down toxins, and your kidneys rid your blood of many waste products and help control the amount of water in your body. The amazing list of unseen and unceasing processes that must go on simultaneously for your body to work properly goes on and on.

Actually, the amazing thing is that many people think that the human body is a product of chance, that we are merely an accident. They believe that our bodies developed on their own as a result of chemical reactions occurring over billions of years through a process called evolution.

Imagine that . . . chemicals combined themselves to become alive, and then the human body, so complicated, so intricate, just assembled itself! Hard to believe, isn't it?

The truth is that we are not an accident. The human body was designed by a Master Designer, the Creator God of the universe. The human body He designed is simple enough that a newborn baby instantly begins making it work and quickly learns the most complex skills. He designed it with sufficient well-orchestrated complexity and built-in control systems so that even before a baby is born the cells in her body are performing chemical reactions she would need a college degree to even begin to understand, and many that the smartest scientists of all are only beginning to discover.

You are marvelously and wonderfully made. Psalm 139:14, says, "I will praise You, for I am fearfully and wonderfully made; marvelous are Your works." As you explore the incredible features of the human body, remember to praise the Creator God who designed the human body and gave one to you.

You will hear from many people that you are nothing more than an animal, a highly evolved one, but an animal nonetheless. This idea comes from people who wrongly believe that life evolved through random processes and all by itself produced increasingly complex animals until humans appeared. They believe that humans are just animals and not special at all. God's Word tells us otherwise.

In Genesis 1:26 it says, "Then God said, 'Let Us make man in Our image, according to Our likeness.'" Therefore, we are not merely animals. God made human beings in His own image.

But you might say, "Well, we look similar to some animals, so aren't we just animals, too?" No, we are not. Humans and some animals do share many similar features, but that does not mean that animals are our ancestors. All it means is that animals and humans were all designed by the same God. We share a common designer, not a common ancestor! A wise master designer would naturally use variations of many common designs in the living things He made.

Just as words are built of letters and books are built from words, so your body is built of organs and tissues, and all the organs and tissues are made of cells. Cells are even called the building blocks of life. We are going to begin exploring the amazing designs of the human body by finding out how the cells of the major organs work.

Anatomy

Anatomy is the study of the body's parts and how they are put together. Anatomy includes how the organs look, where they are, and how everything is connected. Anatomy is the structure of the body. For example, an anatomical study of the circulatory system includes a study of the heart itself and all the blood vessels and their connections to all the other organs.

Anatomy includes not just the things you can see with your eyes, like lungs and kidneys. Anatomy includes the microscopic structures — the cells and the tissues (collections of cells) that make up the larger parts. This study of microscopic anatomy is called histology.

Physiology

Physiology is the study of how the parts of the body function. Physiology is the study of how everything in the body works. For example, physiology of the circulatory system focuses on how the heart works, what controls blood circulation and blood pressure, how oxygen gets into the blood, and how blood delivers oxygen to the tissues and organs.

If we didn't understand some physiology, learning about the human body would just be the dull business of memorizing the names and locations of organs and bones. But when we find out how each part works and interacts with other parts, the study of the human body really does come alive!

Cells and Tissues and Organs, Oh My!

The best way to understand the human body is not just to memorize its parts but to begin with its building blocks and then to see how they form the more complex structures and how they work. We will begin with the most basic building block of the body, the cell. Cells are small but not simple. While cells have a simple list of parts — like nucleus, cytoplasm, and cell membrane — these are subdivided into a dizzying list of smaller parts. Many cells are like tiny factories. There are many types of cells in the body. For example, there are liver cells, muscle cells, kidney cells, nerve cells, skin cells, blood cells — well . . . you get the idea.

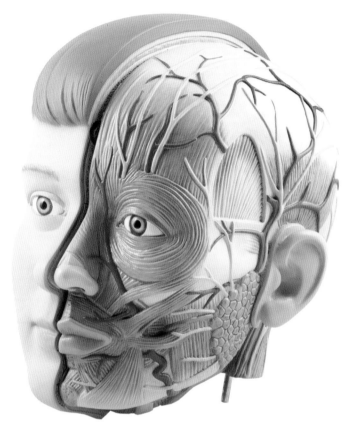

Groups of cells form tissues. Each kind of tissue can be thought of as one of four basic tissue types — epithelial, connective, muscle, and nervous. These tissues cover, connect, move, and communicate. More on that later.

Tissues combine to form more complex structures called organs. Organs are groups of tissues that have a particular function. Lungs, bones, and the brain are examples of organs.

Lastly, we will deal with organ systems. This is where we will "put things together" by exploring groups of organs that work together to do specific things in the body. For example, the bones are all connected together as the skeletal system. And all the parts that process your food — from your mouth and stomach to your liver and intestines — are part of the digestive system.

Before we can put it all together we need to go back to basics, so let's get going with the cell.

2

CELLS

The cell is not only the basic building block of the body but also the basic "functional unit." What does that mean? Well, your body does a lot of things — some things you see and some that you don't. It moves. It grows. It digests food, turning some of it into energy, storing some of it, and discarding the leftovers. It manufactures many kinds of complex chemicals. It tastes, smells, sees, hears, touches, senses temperature, and feels pain. It takes in oxygen from the air and carries it all over your body. It fights infection and protects you from most germs. It stops you from bleeding when you get a cut, and later it heals the cut. All these "functions" are really performed by or inside cells. That's why we say the cell is the smallest "functional unit" of the body. The cell is where the action is!

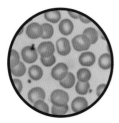
Blood Cell

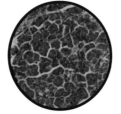
Liver Cell

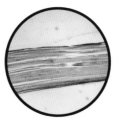
Muscle Cell

Nerve Cell

Nucleus

Cellular Membrane

Blood vessels in embryonic tissue. The vessels are lined by endothelium (simple squamous epithelium) and contain inside immature nucleated red blood cells. (Light microscope micrograph.)

Each cell is like a factory designed to carry out a specific function. There are over 200 different kinds of cells in the human body, and they come in all shapes and sizes. Most cells have three basic parts — a *nucleus* that directs most of the action, a *cell membrane* that forms the cell's outer border, and *cytoplasm* where most of the cell's work gets done. Most kinds of cells have many *organelles* that perform the various jobs in the cell.

Erythrocytes are red blood cells. Their main job is to carry oxygen. Red blood cells are packed with a red oxygen-carrying molecule (hemoglobin), which is why they are red. Erythrocytes are comparatively simple cells. The erythrocytes circulating throughout your body don't even have a nucleus or organelles.

In contrast, liver cells are much more complex. Liver cells process and store nutrients, manufacture important substances, and rid the body of some toxic chemicals. Because liver cells are involved in more complex activities than red blood cells, their structure is more complex.

Each muscle cell is designed to contract, and you can move because muscle cells work together. Certain cells in the pancreas produce *insulin* that controls the amount of sugar in your blood, because either too much or too little is bad for you. Nerve cells transmit nerve impulses so that one part of your body can communicate with another. Otherwise, your hand would not "know" that your brain told it to move. And the list goes on. Each cell has an important job to do.

For all their many differences in structure and function, most cells have a lot of things in common. Here we'll learn about a "typical" cell. Then in our journey through the human body, we will examine specific cell types in more detail.

SO SIMPLE YET *Designed by the Master* SO COMPLEX

Human Cells and Plant Cells

You will soon learn about many different kinds of cells found in the human body. Plants are also made of cells. Plant cells have many things in common with our cells. Plant cells have nuclei containing chromosomes that direct the cellular activities. They have mitochondria and the other organelles we have. And plant cells also have cell membranes.

Plant cell

But plant cells have two things our cells lack — cell walls and chloroplasts. Plant cell membranes are surrounded by a tough cell wall made of cellulose. Humans cannot make cellulose. The cell wall provides a sturdy support for plant cells and helps maintain their shape. Plant cells, unlike our cells, are also able to capture energy directly from sunlight and use it to manufacture sugar. This process is called photosynthesis. Photosynthesis takes place in special organelles called chloroplasts. The chloroplasts in plant cells contain the green pigment chlorophyll, which captures the sun's energy. God designed plant cells to produce sugars and other important foods for humans and animals to eat.

Human cell

Basic Cell Structure

Regardless of size, shape, or complexity, most human cells have, as we mentioned, three main parts. The *cell membrane*, also called the *plasma membrane*, encloses the cell, forming the boundary with its *extracellular* surroundings. One could look at the plasma membrane as the bag or sack that holds all the other parts. This is no ordinary "bag" though. Even the membrane surrounding the cell is specially designed to perform a lot of vital jobs. The cell membrane keeps some things in and keeps other things out, while letting some things travel across it and actively helping other things to pass through. The cell membrane is like the ultimate doorkeeper, and then some!

The control center of the cell is the *nucleus*. It directs the activities of the cell. The nucleus stores all the instructions the cell needs to function. These instructions are in code. The code is written into the structure of DNA, long chain-like molecules that are stored in the nucleus. The blueprint for making each protein the cell it is supposed to make is written in a *gene* in this DNA. Except for mature red blood cells, all cells in the body have at least one nucleus. Some have several *nuclei*.

In between the cell membrane and the nucleus, or nuclei, is the *cytoplasm*. All the parts of the cell that are not part of the nucleus or cell membrane are part of the cytoplasm. Many little "workstations" called *organelles* float in the *cytosol*, which is the cytoplasm's fluid. Dissolved in the cytosol are also many substances like

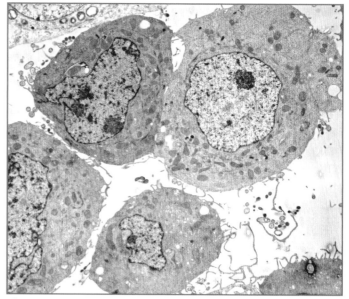
Electron microscopic view of cells

sugars and electrolytes. (*Electrolytes* include sodium ions, potassium ions, calcium ions, and so forth. *Ions* are charged chemicals, and we'll learn later that the way they move into and out of cells is very important.) Large molecules such as enzymes also float around in the cytosol, each doing an important job.

TAKING A CLOSER LOOK
Human Cell Structure

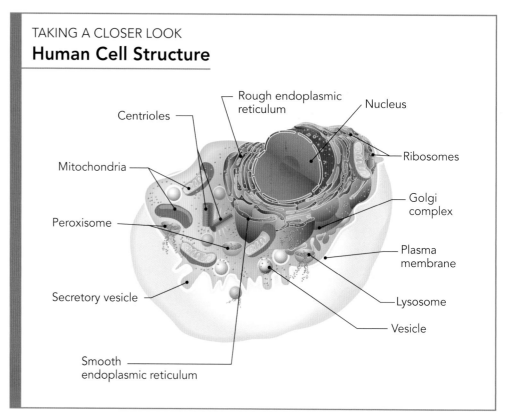

Centrioles

Rough endoplasmic reticulum

Nucleus

Mitochondria

Ribosomes

Peroxisome

Golgi complex

Plasma membrane

Secretory vesicle

Lysosome

Vesicle

Smooth endoplasmic reticulum

The Plasma Membrane

The plasma membrane is the envelope that contains the other components of the cell. Within it is the cytoplasm, its organelles, and the nucleus. Without the plasma membrane, the cell would have no form or structure. The plasma membrane holds the cell together.

However, the plasma membrane is far more than just a container. It helps separate the two major fluid compartments of the body, the *intracellular fluid* — fluid inside cells — from the *extracellular fluid* — fluid that is outside cells. The plasma membrane is also involved in moving fluid, nutrients, and other substances into and out of the cell while forming a barrier to things that should stay out.

Most of the intracellular fluid and most of the extracellular fluid is water, but the concentration of the chemicals dissolved in them makes them very, very different. The chemicals dissolved in these fluids are "water soluble," which means they can dissolve in water. You probably already know that sugar and salt dissolve in water, and oil does not. Well, sugar molecules are water-soluble. Salts are made of ions, like sodium ions and potassium ions and chloride ions, and such salts are also water-soluble. Fats and oils, however, are not water-soluble: they do not dissolve in water. Another name for a fat is *lipid*.

Its Structure

The plasma membrane is actually made up of two layers of molecules. These molecules are called

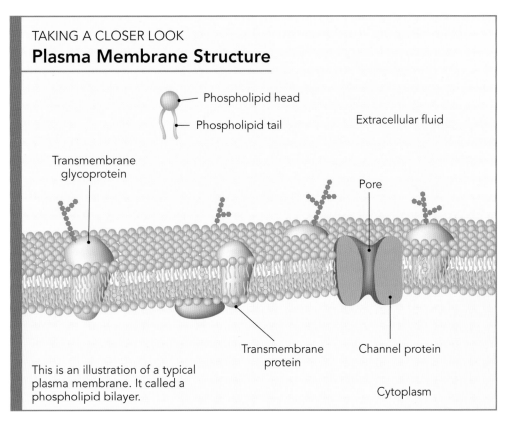

TAKING A CLOSER LOOK
Plasma Membrane Structure

Phospholipid head
Phospholipid tail
Extracellular fluid
Transmembrane glycoprotein
Pore
Transmembrane protein
Channel protein
Cytoplasm

This is an illustration of a typical plasma membrane. It called a phospholipid bilayer.

phospholipids, and they have a very interesting shape, as you can see in the illustration.

These molecules have what can be described as a "head" and two "tails." The "head" of the molecule is charged. This portion of the molecule is water-soluble (known as *hydrophilic*, a word that literally means "water-loving") and is therefore attracted to water. The tail portion is uncharged and avoids water (known as *hydrophobic*, a word that literally means "water-fearing"). These characteristics of phospholipids are important not only in the structure of the plasma membrane, but also for its function.

The plasma membrane is composed of these two layers of phospholipids, creatively called a *phospholipid bilayer*, which means "two layers of phospholipids." The phospholipid molecules are lying with the heads facing the outer and inner surface of the plasma membrane and the tails pointing to the interior of the membrane. The hydrophilic (water-loving) heads of the molecules are in contact with the watery fluid inside and outside the cells. The hydrophobic (water "fearing") tails are pointing toward each other, as far from the watery fluids as possible. This helps maintain the integrity of the membrane.

In addition to the phospholipids, the plasma membrane has a lot of protein molecules embedded in it. Some of these proteins extend completely through the plasma membrane. Some are only attached to its inner or outer surface. These proteins are vital to the normal function of the cell. Some of them ferry certain substances across the membrane. Some form a doorway allowing particular sorts of molecules to pass through. Some of them are like name tags that identify the cell to other cells. Some even form attachments to other neighboring cells.

Its Function

So beyond just holding the contents of the cell in one container, what is the function of the plasma membrane? Well, among other things, it helps regulate what goes into and out of the cell.

Some substances, like water and certain lipid (fat) molecules, can pass directly through the plasma membrane and get into or out of the cell. However, many other substances cannot easily get into cells. Often, these can gain access to the cell by means of some of the proteins in the plasma membrane. These special proteins have a channel in them to allow things into a cell that could not pass directly through the plasma membrane.

Some things, however, are too large even for protein channels. So in the case of the largest molecules, there is a special mechanism called *endocytosis*. In this case, a portion of the plasma membrane folds into the cell, surrounds the molecules needed, and then the membrane pinches off, forming a small bubble-like *vesicle*, which is then processed inside the cell. Occasionally this process is reversed and vesicles formed within the cell merge with the plasma membrane and release products made by the cell. The process of releasing material from inside the cell is called *exocytosis*.

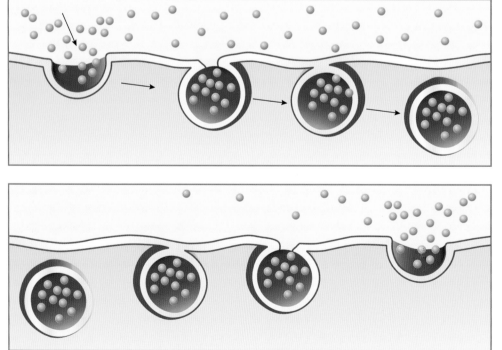

Vesicles can transport material into and out of cells. During endocytosis, shown on top, material is transported into a cell by packaging it into a vesicle. Exocytosis is shown in the bottom illustration. There, a vesicle merges with the cell membrane and the material it contains is released.

Further, the plasma membrane is able to respond to cellular signals because of some of the proteins on its outer surface. These proteins bind to certain molecules that cause the cell to react in a specific way.

There are also special proteins on the outer surface of the plasma membrane that help identify the cell. In other words, these proteins are like an identification tag for the cell, so the body itself can know which cells are which. When we study the immune system, you will see this in action. So the plasma membrane isn't just any old bag, is it?

Cell Markers

The plasma membrane contains some special proteins called glycoproteins. These proteins have carbohydrate (sugar) groups attached that protrude into the extracellular fluid. These carbohydrate groups along with other special molecules called glycolipids form a coating on the cell surface known as the glycocalyx.

The pattern of the glycocalyx varies from cell to cell. It is distinctive enough that it forms a molecular "signature" for a cell. This is one way that cells can recognize one another.

Cytosol

Cytosol is the liquid found inside the cell. It surrounds the organelles and the nucleus. The *cytosol* plus the *organelles* make up the *cytoplasm*.

The cytosol is mostly water. Water makes up 70 to 75 percent of the volume of the cell. The cytosol contains many substances, and the cell works hard to maintain the appropriate balance of the substances found there.

There are lots of ions (charged atoms or molecules) in the cytosol, mostly potassium, sodium, chloride, and bicarbonate ions. These ions help maintain the electrical balance between the inside and outside of the cell (called the *membrane potential*, as we will explore later), as well as help

maintain the correct water concentration inside the cell.

The cytosol also contains lots of proteins and *amino acids*. (Amino acids are the building blocks of proteins; we'll get more into that later.) These proteins and amino acids provide the raw materials for many of the activities of the cell.

Endoplasmic Reticulum

The *endoplasmic reticulum* is a network of tubes and membranes that is connected to the nuclear membrane. The endoplasmic reticulum, or ER, comes in two forms, *rough ER* and *smooth ER*.

Rough ER is bumpy because it is covered with *ribosomes*. Ribosomes are little factories for making protein. Rough ER is primarily involved with protein production. Proteins that are made in the ribosomes can be modified by the endoplasmic reticulum to fit them for their particular jobs. The particular proteins and lipids that make up the plasma membrane are made in the rough ER.

TAKING A CLOSER LOOK
Endoplasmic Reticulum

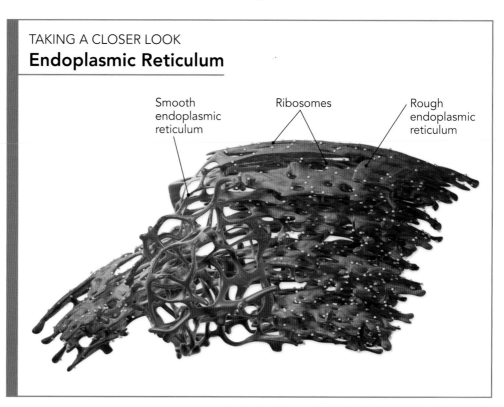

Smooth endoplasmic reticulum

Ribosomes

Rough endoplasmic reticulum

Smooth ER is more tube-like in appearance and is not covered with ribosomes. It is more involved with production of fats, certain hormones, and the breakdown of some toxins that enter the cell.

Golgi Apparatus

The Golgi apparatus is a collection of small flattened sacs that stack on one another. They tend to be flatter in the middle and more rounded on the ends.

Cells produce lots of things, especially fats and proteins. The Golgi apparatus helps the cell transport these products to where they are needed. It does this by forming little sacs, or vesicles, around the needed items. These vesicles pinch off from the Golgi apparatus and travel to their destination. Sometimes this is within the cell itself. Sometimes the vesicle moves to the plasma membrane and releases its contents outside the cell via *exocytosis*.

The Golgi apparatus is an exquisitely designed delivery system. Without it, the cell could not function.

Lysosomes

Lysosomes are small vesicles containing enzymes that can digest many kinds of molecules and debris. This may seem surprising. After all, aren't these types of substances dangerous to the cell itself? Yes, they can be, but they are still very necessary.

Lysosomes break down worn-out organelles, bacteria, and toxic substances. For example, white blood cells contain a large number of lysosomes. That is how they are able to help rid the body of invading bacteria.

Lysosomes also aid the cell by breaking down substances the cell needs for nutrition, particularly large molecules the cell takes in. In fact, the

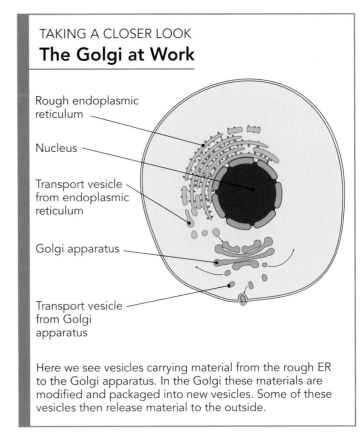

TAKING A CLOSER LOOK
The Golgi at Work

Rough endoplasmic reticulum

Nucleus

Transport vesicle from endoplasmic reticulum

Golgi apparatus

Transport vesicle from Golgi apparatus

Here we see vesicles carrying material from the rough ER to the Golgi apparatus. In the Golgi these materials are modified and packaged into new vesicles. Some of these vesicles then release material to the outside.

lysosome is sometimes called the "stomach" of the cell. And by breaking down organelles that are worn out or no longer needed, the lysosomes recycle valuable materials.

Ribosomes

Ribosomes are found floating in the cytoplasm and attached to the rough endoplasmic reticulum. These are little structures, but they have a very big job. *Ribosomes* are where proteins are made. Let's consider where a ribosome gets its protein-building instructions.

You may remember that the nucleus of a cell directs the cell's activities. The instructions for what the cell is supposed to do are stored in the nucleus. The "blueprints" for how to build the proteins a cell is supposed to build are mostly stored in the nucleus. These "blueprints" or "recipes" for building proteins are called genes.

TAKING A CLOSER LOOK
Ribosomes

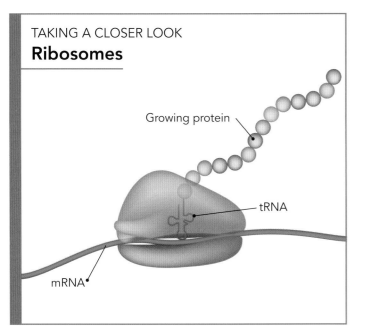

Growing protein

tRNA

mRNA

Genes with protein-building instructions are in the nucleus, but the protein-making ribosomes are located in the cytoplasm. How can the ribosomes get their instructions? Well, copies of the instructions, called *messenger RNA*, are made in the nucleus. Those messages move from the nucleus into the cytoplasm. There, ribosomes read the messenger RNA's instructions and build the protein described, stitching together a string of *amino acids*, which are the building blocks of proteins. The ribosome follows the "recipe" stored in the nucleus and copied onto messenger RNA.

Mitochondria

The *mitochondria* are often called the "powerhouses" of the cell. They are called that because they generate and store energy. Mitochondria are like super battery chargers.

These are elongated bean-shaped structures with lots of folded membranes inside. Unlike the other organelles in the cell, mitochondria even contain some genes used to reproduce themselves! (Remember, all the rest of the genes in your body's cells are stored in the nuceli.)

The mitochondria are responsible for producing high-energy molecules. Those high-energy molecules are like batteries: they store energy until the cell needs the energy for something. One of the most important high-energy molecules is ATP (which stands for *adenosine triphosphate*, if you want to show off to your friends . . .). This molecule stores energy needed to fuel cellular activities.

ATP is actually built from ADP, *adenosine diphosphate*. ADP is like a battery that needs to be recharged. And ATP is like a fully charged battery. As you might guess from the names *triphosphate* and *biphosphate*, ATP contains three "phosphates" and ADP contains two "phosphates." The bonds that hold phosphate onto ADP and ATP store a lot of energy,

TAKING A CLOSER LOOK
Mitochondria

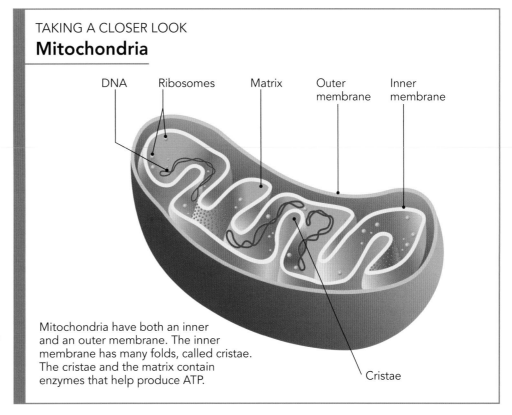

DNA   Ribosomes   Matrix   Outer membrane   Inner membrane

Mitochondria have both an inner and an outer membrane. The inner membrane has many folds, called cristae. The cristae and the matrix contain enzymes that help produce ATP.

Cristae

SO SIMPLE YET SO COMPLEX — Designed by the Master

Making Mitochondria

The nucleus is not the only place that DNA is found in the cell. Mitochondria have multiple copies of their own DNA. This DNA exists as a circular molecule containing 37 genes. Interestingly enough, mitochondrial DNA is inherited only from the mother. In addition, mitochondria contain RNA and ribosomes. During times of increased energy needs, the mitochondria can reproduce themselves to increase their number. They grow and divide by pinching in half.

much like a battery stores energy until it is needed. When energy is needed, a high-energy bond in ATP (or in other similar high-energy molecules) is broken and the energy released from it is used to power whatever the cell needs to do.

But where does the mitochondria get the energy to charge these chemical batteries? After all, you've learned before that energy cannot be created or destroyed but only transformed from one form to another. The fuel that provides the energy for the mitochondria's charging operation comes from sugar.

The process of providing energy to the cell is kind of like putting wood in a stove or putting gasoline in a car. Wood and gasoline are both fuels. The wood in the stove burns to make heat that can be used to cook food or heat your home. The gasoline in a car is burned by the engine and provides energy to make the car move. It is not all that different to make energy for a cell. The cell's favorite fuel is not wood or gasoline but the sugar *glucose*. The energy produced when it is *metabolized* — a sort of very controlled way of "burning" the fuel — must be captured and stored in chemical "batteries" like ATP.

Remember, think of ATP and ADP like rechargeable batteries. The primary fuel for cells is the sugar glucose. Glucose is taken into the mitochondria through a series of chemical reactions, and the molecule ATP is produced by recharging ADP with energy from glucose. Just as burning wood or gasoline depends on oxygen, this chain of chemical reactions in the mitochondria also requires oxygen (so thank your lungs here!).

The number of mitochondria in a cell depends on the energy needs of the cell. Liver cells, for example, are involved in making proteins, making cholesterol and other lipids (fats), making and secreting bile, and many other things. So you may well imagine that it takes lots of energy to perform all these functions. In fact, a liver cell can have as many as 2,000 mitochondria!

Centrosome and Cytoskeleton

You might ask yourself, "What keeps all this stuff in place?" Well, there is an answer! The cell has a sort

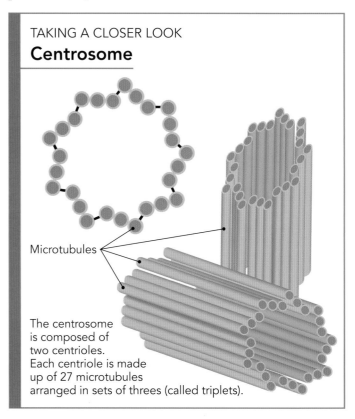

TAKING A CLOSER LOOK
Centrosome

Microtubules

The centrosome is composed of two centrioles. Each centriole is made up of 27 microtubules arranged in sets of threes (called triplets).

of skeleton, called a cytoskeleton, that helps with that task. This cytoskeleton is composed of a network of tubes and filaments that run throughout the cell. Though not pictured in most diagrams of cells, these fine tubes and filaments provide support for the organelles.

But this support system does more than just hold things in one place. Along with the cytoskeleton, there are special motor proteins that help organelles move around. Mitochondria, lysosomes, and vesicles all move around the cell with the help of these amazing structures.

Another very special organelle, called the *centrosome*, is necessary for cellular reproduction. After all, most kinds of cells wear out and must therefore reproduce, or duplicate, themselves. We'll go into the complex process of how a cell divides in two later.

Sometimes it seems like all the action is in the nucleus when we talk about cell division. But if it weren't for the centrosome, which is located outside the nucleus in the cytoplasm, cellular reproduction would be a disorganized chaotic mess. Nothing would end up in the right place!

The centrosome is an L-shaped structure made up of two barrel-shaped *centrioles*. These centrioles are responsible for helping form a complex of *micro-tubules*, called the *mitotic spindle*, which guides the cell's chromosomes during cell division.

Nucleus

The nucleus is the control center of the cell. Stored in the DNA (deoxyribonucleic acid) in each cell's nucleus are the genetic instructions needed to make all the proteins in the body. The genes — the little recipes for building proteins — and even the regulations that determine how and when those genes are to be used are part of the DNA. The nucleus regulates the types of proteins made by its cell and their

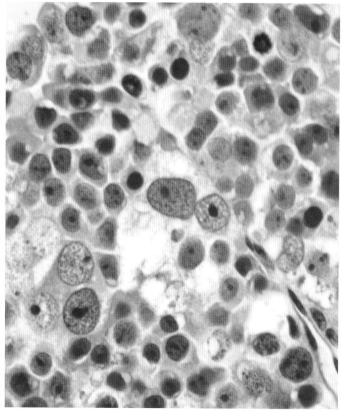

Micrograph of a spermatocytic seminoma

amounts. Even though the nucleus contains a copy of your entire *genome*, only the information needed by each cell type is ever turned on and used.

The majority of cells have one nucleus. However, there are exceptions. Skeletal muscle cells (and a few other cell types) have more than one nucleus, and mature human red blood cells have none.

Just as the cell has a cell membrane, so the nucleus has a *nuclear membrane*. You recall that messages — in the form of messenger RNA — must pass from the nucleus into the cytoplasm to deliver instructions to the ribosomes. Did you wonder how the message gets through? Well, the outer part of the nuclear membrane connects to rough endoplasmic retic-ulum. Through tiny pores in the nuclear membrane, substances can pass from the nucleus into the cytoplasm. That way the instructions from the nucleus can reach the cytoplasm where they can be implemented.

DNA

DNA — deoxyribonucleic acid — is one of the most amazing molecules in the universe. In your DNA is contained all the information needed to make your body!

DNA is a big molecule made up of two long strings of smaller molecules called *nucleotides*. There are four different kinds of nucleotides present in DNA. These four nucleotides are the building blocks of DNA. Two long strands of nucleotides are attracted to each other and form a structure that looks like a twisted ladder. That structure is called a *double helix*.

So what is so amazing about long strings of chemicals?

Well, it turns out that the order in which the nucleotides are found in DNA is very, very important. Those four nucleotides in DNA aren't just DNA's building blocks. They are the "letters" in a code — the genetic code of life that is used not only in the human body but in all the living things God designed!

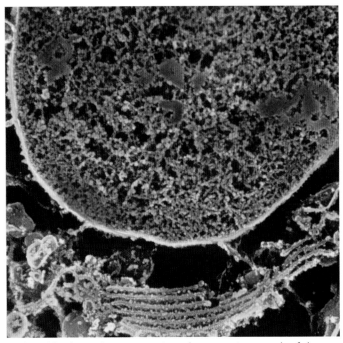

Colored high resolution scanning electron micrograph of the nucleus and rough endoplasmic reticulum of a primordial testis germ cell.

You see, DNA is not just a string of chemicals. It is a very complex system of information! For decades now, scientists have studied the "letters" and "words" in the DNA and how they work.

Imagine each nucleotide as a "letter." Three "letters" form a "word." And a group of "words" can give coded instructions for building a protein or even for regulating how those instructions are carried out. The DNA in a human cell contains over 3 billion nucleotides. The instructions coded in your DNA determine which proteins can be made.

Each section of DNA that has the information for a particular protein is called a "gene." Another way of looking at this is to think of a certain group of nucleotide "words" combining to make up a genetic "book." Other sets of nucleotide words make up other books, and so on.

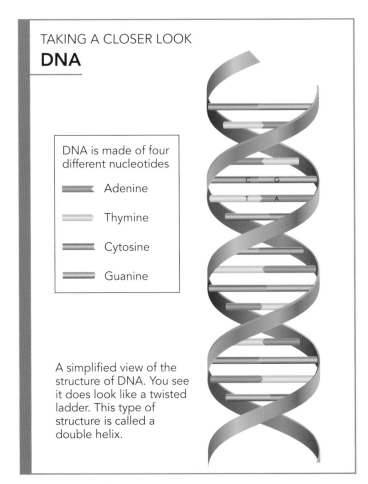

TAKING A CLOSER LOOK

DNA

DNA is made of four different nucleotides

Adenine

Thymine

Cytosine

Guanine

A simplified view of the structure of DNA. You see it does look like a twisted ladder. This type of structure is called a double helix.

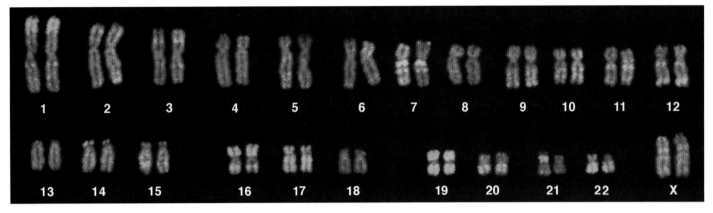

This is a picture of a person's chromosomes. As you can see, humans have 23 pairs of chromosomes. The autosomal chromosomes are numbered according to their length. Number one is the longest and number 22 is the shortest. The remaining pair are the sex chromosomes.

However, DNA also contains coded instructions for other things, like the directions for what kind of cell each cell is supposed to be or how busy it is supposed to be. Some scientists have claimed that the DNA that didn't code for proteins was leftover evolutionary junk with no purpose. Bible-believing scientists know that evolution did not create life, DNA, or the human body. Therefore, these scientists predicted that none of our DNA was evolutionary "junk." Now, scientists have begun finding that "junk" DNA really does have a purpose. The double-helix structure of DNA was discovered in 1953, but scientists are just beginning to figure out how much coded information is contained in each molecule of DNA.

So each strand of DNA is made up of many, many genes. Each gene gives the instructions for building a protein. Proteins are built out of amino acids. Proteins are a kind of biological molecule, and they do much of the "work" in your body. Lots of molecules you may have heard of are proteins. *Enzymes* that perform all the chemical reactions in your cells, *antibodies* that fight infectious invaders, *taste receptors* in your tongue, *collagen* that holds much of your body together, the *actin* and *myosin* molecules that make your muscles contract, the *clotting factors* that make your blood clot, and the transport proteins and identification proteins embedded in your cell

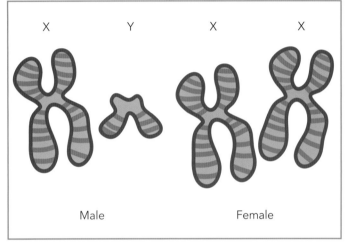

The sex chromosomes determine whether a person is male or female. A person who has an XY pair is male. Those who have an XX pair are female.

TAKING A CLOSER LOOK
Genes and Chromosomes

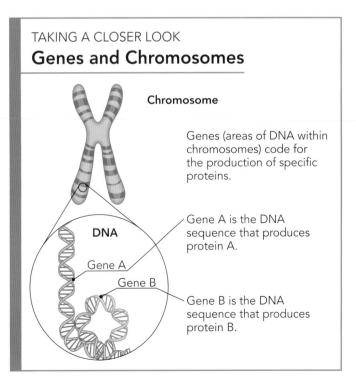

Chromosome

Genes (areas of DNA within chromosomes) code for the production of specific proteins.

Gene A is the DNA sequence that produces protein A.

Gene B is the DNA sequence that produces protein B.

DNA

Gene A

Gene B

membranes are all proteins. Each and every protein molecule must be built in a cell, following the instructions from the nucleus.

Each double helix molecule of DNA is carefully organized and packaged into a chromosome. Each *chromosome* is like a section of a huge library where lots of books are stored. A chromosome consists of DNA — like the books — and special proteins that help package it and take care of it — like "shelves." Human beings have 46 chromosomes in each of the body cells.

The DNA in one of your cells would be about 6 feet long if it were stretched out. In just this tiny strand of DNA is contained enough information to fill hundreds of books, and the DNA in just one of your cells contains the coded information to build your whole body!

DNA at Work

So what exactly does DNA do?

DNA Can Make Proteins

We said that DNA was more than just a string of molecules. It is a complex system of information. This information is used primarily to make the proteins in our body.

Proteins are one of the most important substances in the body. Proteins are made up of long chains of molecules called *amino acids*. For proteins to function properly, the order of these amino acid building blocks must be correct. So there must be a very precise process to make proteins.

TAKING A CLOSER LOOK
Building a Protein

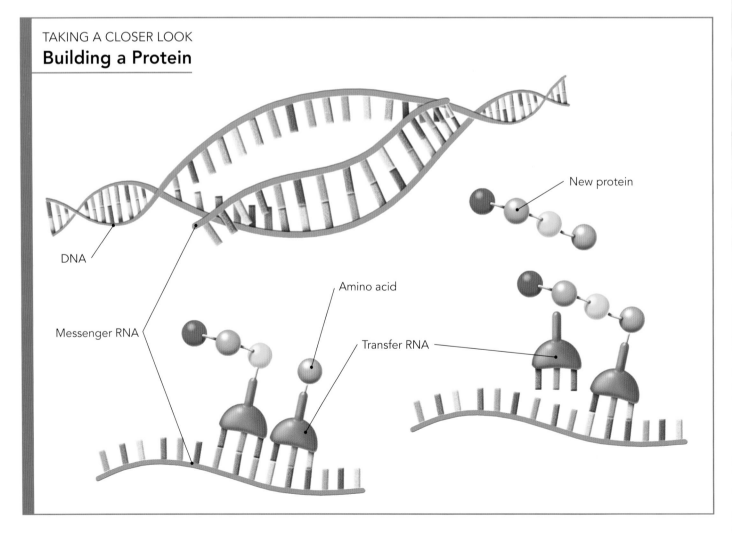

DNA

Messenger RNA

Amino acid

Transfer RNA

New protein

The process of protein making is incredible. DNA uncoils and exposes the gene that contains the necessary instructions. Then the particular segment of the DNA "ladder" that contains the information about the protein splits to expose its nucleotides. (Remember the "words" and "letters"!) Then these nucleotide "words" are read and a special molecule is made. This special molecule is called messenger RNA (mRNA). The mRNA takes the information from the DNA and leaves the nucleus through the pores in the nuclear membrane. Outside the nucleus, the mRNA connects to ribosomes.

Once they're on a ribosome, the mRNA is "read" by another type of RNA, called *transfer RNA* (tRNA). Each kind of tRNA carries the code for a particular amino acid and an attachment for that amino acid. As each segment of the mRNA is read, the tRNA brings the correct amino acid, in the correct order, and the protein is assembled. The ribosome stitches together each protein, folding it carefully so that it will work just right.

What Is "Junk DNA"?

Only a small portion of our DNA actually contains the information that codes for proteins. So what, then, is the purpose of the rest of our DNA?

Many scientists over the last few decades have felt that if any portion of DNA did not actually code for proteins, it had no purpose. For that reason, many scientists began to refer to this part of our DNA as "junk DNA." They felt that these useless regions of DNA were merely left over from our evolutionary past.

However, in recent years, it has been shown that junk DNA is not junk at all. These regions of our DNA are quite active and serve many functions, such as helping switch genes on and off. Every day, researchers are discovering more about how "junk DNA" actually works!

You see, our Master Designer does not make "junk!"

Do Humans and Chimps Have Similar DNA?

It is often said that the DNA of humans and chimps are 98 percent alike. This popular notion has been repeated and repeated so often that most people believe it to be true. Many scientists promote this idea to support their mistaken idea that humans and chimps evolved from a common ancestor a few million years ago. This supposed similarity in DNA is used as "proof" of an evolutionary link between humans and chimps.

Actually, when you really examine the data, you find that the similarity between human and chimp DNA is more like 70 percent. It is nowhere near the 98 percent that some people claim.

Even though there is a 70 percent similarity, that 30 percent difference means an awful lot. Between humans and chimps there are millions and millions of sequences in the DNA that are different. That is obvious as humans and chimps are distinctly different creatures.

So how can we explain the 70 percent of our DNA that is similar to the chimp's? This is simple for the Christian. We understand that all living things have a common Designer, not a common ancestor, as evolution would suggest. This amazing Designer would allow for many design similarities in the creatures he created. These similar features would be reflected in similarities in our DNA.

This process occurs thousand of times each second, and countless proteins are made in our cells each day.

If that were all DNA could do, it would be amazing. But there's more. . . .

DNA Can Make DNA

Well, DNA is able (with the help of a series of proteins and enzymes) to reproduce itself. By doing this, the information contained in the DNA can be passed on when the cell divides.

It works like this.

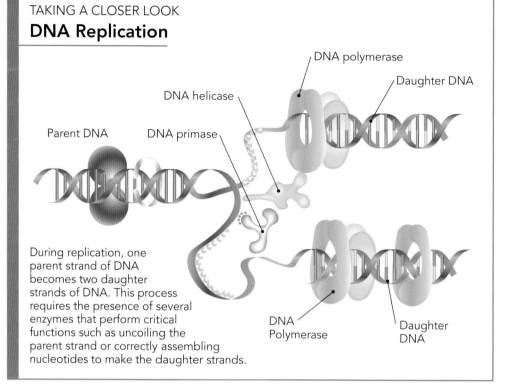

TAKING A CLOSER LOOK
DNA Replication

DNA polymerase

Daughter DNA

DNA helicase

Parent DNA

DNA primase

During replication, one parent strand of DNA becomes two daughter strands of DNA. This process requires the presence of several enzymes that perform critical functions such as uncoiling the parent strand or correctly assembling nucleotides to make the daughter strands.

DNA Polymerase

Daughter DNA

You have seen that DNA looks sort of like a twisted ladder. When it is time for a cell to divide, the membrane around the nucleus temporarily dissolves and the DNA duplicates itself.

First, the DNA in each chromosome uncoils. Then it splits into two strands (almost as if the rungs of the ladder were split in two). With the help of a special set of enzymes, each strand of DNA is copied. When the process is finished, there are two complete sets of chromosomes where there was one set before. Each set of chromosomes is then placed in the newly formed nucleus of a new "daughter cell."

How Cells Divide

While we are on the subject, let's take a closer look at how cells divide. After all, we continually need more cells as we grow and worn-out cells need to be replaced. How does this happen? Let's explore the cell cycle and see how this works! The *cell cycle* is sort of like the life cycle of a cell. There is a time for a cell to focus on its job, whatever that happens to be. And then for most kinds of cells there is a time for it to copy itself and become two "daughter cells."

The part of the cell cycle when a cell is not actually splitting into two cells is called *interphase*. That's when a cell simply does its job, or jobs. During this time, most of the protein-making activity of the cell occurs. The substances that the cell makes for the body's use are manufactured during interphase. Also, during interphase more organelles are made so that there are enough to supply both daughter cells after division. Near the end of interphase, the cell prepares to divide. The DNA in the nucleus duplicates during this part of interphase. For a short period of time, then, the cell has twice its normal amount of DNA — 46 *pairs* of chromosomes rather than just 46 chromosomes! Because these duplicated chromosomes are stuck together, we often use another name to describe them here — a *chromatid*. A chromosome and its copy, stuck together, is called *a pair of sister chromatids*. Remember, the DNA gets duplicated during interphase so that it is all ready to be split between the two new cells that will be formed during cell division.

The part of the cell cycle that is directly involved with dividing the cell into two daughter cells is called *mitosis*. So the working phase of a cell's cycle is interphase, and the dividing phase of a cell's cycle is mitosis. Mitosis can be broken down into four steps, called phases (wouldn't you just know it . . .). We will examine each in turn.

The first phase of mitosis is called *prophase*. Remember that the DNA gets duplicated before interphase is over. That DNA is a tangled mess like spaghetti, however, and it must be sorted out before the chromosomes can be assigned to each daughter cell. During prophase, the DNA coils and tightens, or *condenses*, so that the chromosomes are dark enough to be visible under a microscope.

Remember the centrioles in the cytoplasm? Well the membrane around the nucleus dissolves, allowing

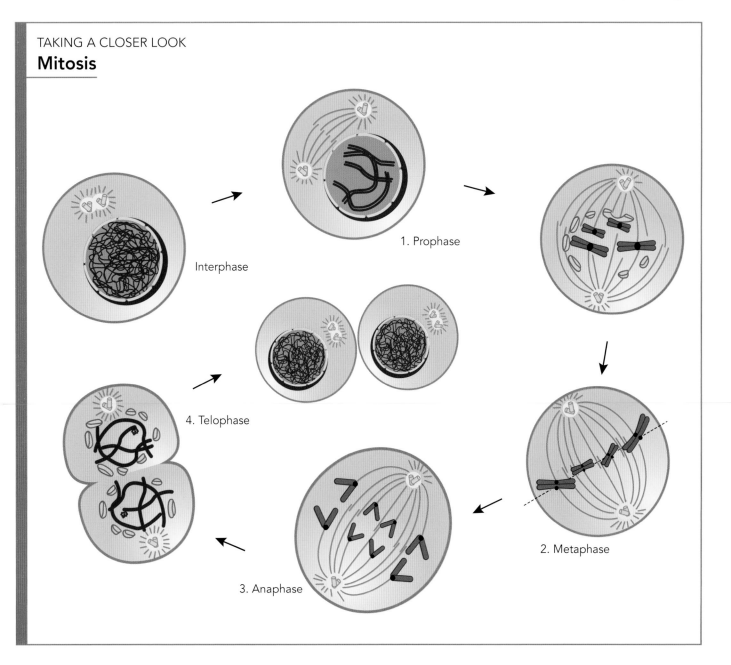

TAKING A CLOSER LOOK
Mitosis

Interphase

1. Prophase

2. Metaphase

3. Anaphase

4. Telophase

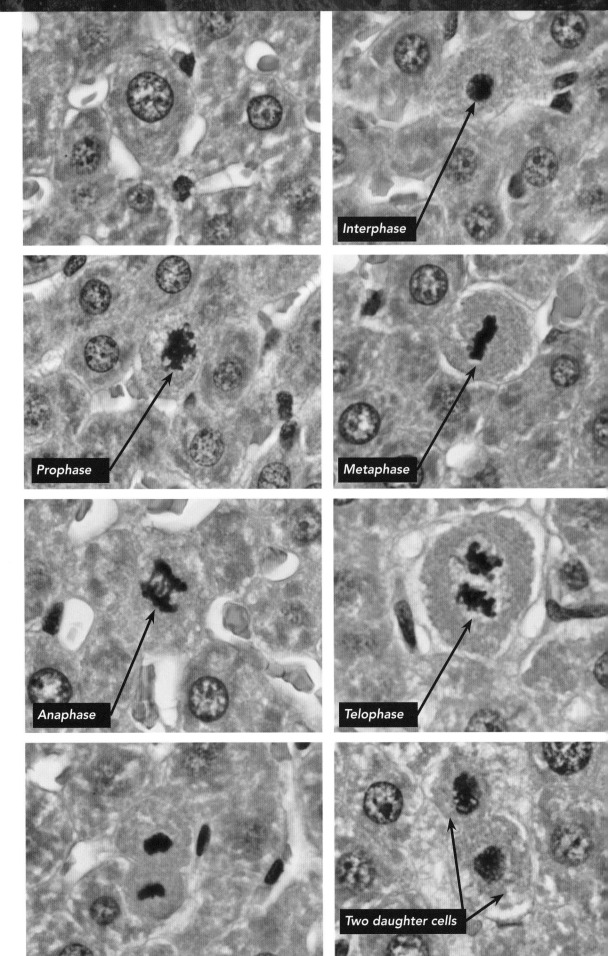

Interphase

Prophase

Metaphase

Anaphase

Telophase

Two daughter cells

Hepatocytes (liver cells) undergoing mitosis

the centrioles to build a scaffold on which the chromosomes can be organized. The centrioles separate, moving to opposite ends of the cell. A series of microtubules form and anchor to the centrioles. These microtubules attach to the duplicated chromosome pairs — *the sister chromatids* — and begin moving them to the center of the cell.

When all the chromosomes, traveling along the microtubules strung between the centrioles, arrive at the center of the cell, the cell is in *metaphase*. Metaphase is the second phase of mitosis.

The third phase is called *anaphase*. This is the shortest phase of mitosis. At this time, the sister chromatids are pulled apart, each chromatid, or chromosome, moving to opposite ends of the cell. Anaphase ends when the chromosomes reach opposite poles of the cell. Now there is a complete complement of genetic material, enough for one new cell, gathered together. Because the sister chromatids stayed attached to each other until they were all lined up in the middle, and then were pulled apart in opposite directions, each daughter cell should contain identical copies of the genes in the original "parent" cell.

The final phase of mitosis is called *telophase*. During this phase, the chromosomes uncoil and become much less visible. New nuclear membranes form at each end of the cell, encircling the group of chromosomes. Thus, for a brief time the cell has two nuclei (each identical to the original nucleus in the parent cell). Then the cell pinches off in the center, forming two daughter cells.

Moving On . . .

So we have taken a look at the cell and its parts. It is difficult to imagine how people can call the cell "simple," because it certainly isn't. As we continue our journey exploring the human body, there will be many examples of the complex functions performed by cells.

Is DNA Just an Accident?

Many people think so. One common evolutionary belief is that millions of years ago, DNA just formed itself from chemicals, building the complex DNA molecule itself as well as the complex coded messages in it.

You see, many people believe that millions of years ago there was no life on earth. They believe earth's oceans were full of chemicals that, all by themselves, formed the nucleotides from which DNA is made. Then they believe DNA assembled itself from the nucleotides. Yep, they believe that strands of DNA, millions of nucleotides long, just came together . . . in exactly the right order . . . by chance.

But even if that could happen — and nothing in science has ever discovered any way that it could — the evolutionary story still wouldn't make sense. After all, DNA is not just a string of chemicals; it is a very complex information system. So even if DNA could have assembled itself, where did the coded language contained in the DNA come from? Without a source of information and a language code to record that information, the nucleotides in DNA really would just be a string of nonsensical chemicals. You see, information does not come from matter. Information only comes from a higher source of information. And who is the highest source of information?

DNA is not the result of random chance processes. It is another testimony to the magnificent Creator God, the source of all information.

3

TISSUES

As we have seen, cells are marvelously complex. They can do amazing things. However, one cell cannot do the work of many cells. A group of cells that perform similar or related functions is called a tissue. Tissues have many functions, but there are really only four basic categories of tissues. All tissues in the body belong to one of these four groups. These tissue types are epithelial tissue, muscle tissue, connective tissue, and nervous tissue. In a nutshell, they cover, move, connect, and communicate, but that description barely scratches the surface. Let's explore each type in turn.

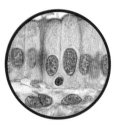
Epithelial Tissue

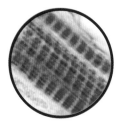
Muscle Tissue

Connective Tissue

Nervous Tissue

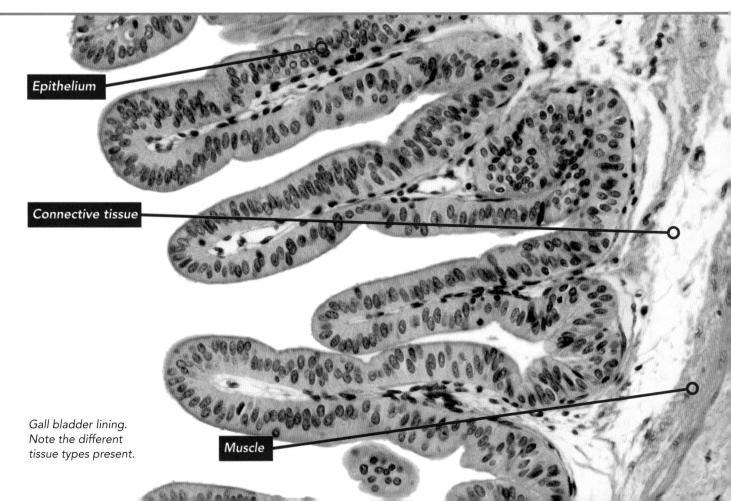

Epithelium

Connective tissue

Muscle

Gall bladder lining. Note the different tissue types present.

Epithelial tissue (or epithelium) lines your body cavities or covers surfaces. For example, you may have heard that your skin has layers of cells. Well, the outer layer of skin is an epithelial layer, called epidermis. The sheets of cells that line the stomach and intestines, as well as the cells that line the heart, blood vessels, and the lungs are also kinds of epithelial tissue. As you might imagine, the epithelial tissues in each of these locations differ a great deal, but they cover surfaces or line cavities or tubes. They are all in the category called epithelium.

Epithelial tissue is specialized to perform many activities. It can act as a barrier for protection. For example, your skin keeps out bacteria, and it is waterproof! The lining of the digestive tract is designed to absorb water and many kinds of molecules, then digestive enzymes break down your food. The epithelium of the kidneys helps rid the body of waste products. Your hair follicles are a specialized kind of epithelium that grows hair!

Another very special type of epithelial tissue is called glandular epithelium. This tissue forms the glands of the body. Glands are groups of cells that produce and secrete certain substances. (Some of

TAKING A CLOSER LOOK
Types of Epithelial Tissue Cells

Cells	Location	Function
Simple squamous	Air sacs of lungs and the lining of the heart, blood vessels, and lymphatic vessels.	Allows materials to pass through by diffusion and filtration, and secretes lubricating substance.
Stratified squamous	Lines the esophagus, mouth, and vagina.	Protects against abrasion.
Simple cuboidal	In ducts and secretory portions of small glands and in kidney tubules.	Secretes and absorbs.
Transitional	Lines the bladder, uretha, and the ureters.	Allows the urinary organs to expand and stretch.
Simple columnar	Ciliated tissues are in bronchi, uterine tubes, and uterus; smooth (nonciliated tissues) are in the digestive tract, bladder.	Absorbs; it also secretes mucous and enzymes.
Pseudostratified columnar	Ciliated tissue lines the trachea and much of the upper respiratory tract.	Secretes mucus; ciliated tissue moves mucus.

these are used in the body, and some are discharged outside the body or even into the cavities and tubes that they line.) We will learn much about glands as we study the various body systems.

Muscle tissue is responsible for movement. Muscles move large parts of your body, like your legs and your fingers. Muscle tissue also moves your stomach's walls to churn your food, and muscle tissue moves to guide food through your digestive tract. Another kind of muscle tissue moves to keep the heart pumping, and still other muscles work together to help your lungs draw in air!

Even though there are several kinds of muscle tissue, each is made of muscle cells. Muscle cells contain structures called *myofilaments* that allow the cells to contract. A little muscle contraction gives you

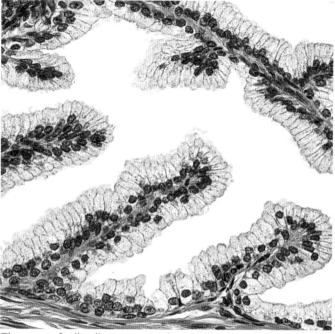

The rows of tall cells you see in this photomicrograph are epithelial tissue.

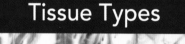

Tissue Types

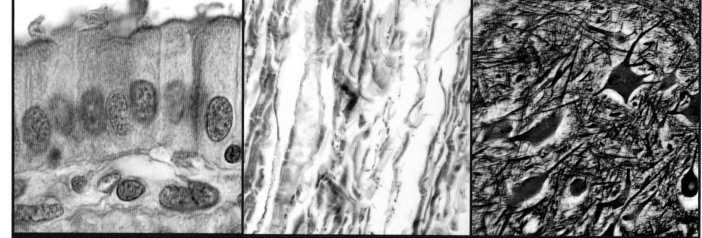

Epithelial Tissue

Epithelial tissue (or epithelium) lines body cavities or covers surfaces. For example, the outer layer of skin is epithelium. The sheet of cells that line the stomach and intestines, as well as the cells that line the heart, blood vessels, and the lungs, is epithelial tissue.

Connective Tissue

Connective tissue helps provide a framework for the body. It also helps connect and support other organs in the body. Further, it helps insulate the body, and it even helps transport substances throughout the body. This tissue can be hard or soft. Some connective tissue stretches. One type is even fluid. Connective tissue is comprised of three parts: cells, fibers, and ground substance.

Nerve Tissue

Nervous tissue is the primary component of the nervous system. The nervous system regulates and controls bodily functions.

Nerve cells are incredible. They are able to receive signals or input from other cells, generate a nerve impulse, and transmit a signal to other nerve cells or organs.

muscle tone so you don't flop like a rag doll. A little more muscle contraction produces movement.

There are three types of muscle tissue.

Skeletal muscle is attached to the bones of the skeleton. When it contracts, it allows us to move our arms and legs, or grasp something with our hands, or smile when we're happy. This type of muscle contracts when we want it to; it is under our conscious control. That is why it is often referred to as voluntary muscle. The distinctively striped cellular structure of skeletal muscle, easily seen under the microscope, differs from that of other types of muscle. The skeletal muscle cells are usually arranged neatly side by side so that they can all pull in the same direction.

SO SIMPLE YET Designed by the Master SO COMPLEX

Did you know that you are constantly shedding your skin? Your skin contains many layers of cells. The bottom layer of cells multiplies rapidly. Crowded out by newer cells, older cell layers are pushed upward. Meanwhile, many of these cells produce a protein called keratin. Your hair and nails are also made of keratin produced by the cells in your hair follicles and nail beds, so you can imagine that keratin molecules are tough. Keratin-producing cells in your skin gradually fill with keratin as they age and are pushed closer and closer to the surface of your skin. By the time they near the surface, these skin cells die and leave behind the keratin they contained as part of a waterproof protective layer on the surface of your skin. This layer is constantly rubbed away by your day-to-day activities but is quickly replaced.

Muscle Tissue Types

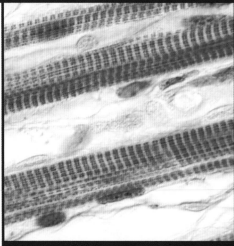

Skeletal Muscle Tissue

Skeletal muscle is attached to the bones of the skeleton. When it contracts, it allows us to move our arms and legs, or grasp something with our hands, or smile when we're happy. It has a structure that is distinct from other types of muscle as we will see.

Smooth Muscle Tissue

Smooth muscle is found in the walls of most of the hollow organs of the body. For example, it is found in the walls of our digestive tract where it helps push our food as it is digested. Smooth muscle is found in blood vessels, the urinary tract, the respiratory tract, the prostate, among other places. Smooth muscle is not under our direct control, and is sometimes referred to as involuntary muscle.

Cardiac Muscle

The third type of smooth muscle is cardiac muscle. It is found only in the walls of the heart. This type of muscle is also an involuntary muscle.

Smooth muscle is found in the walls of most of the hollow organs of the body. In the walls of our digestive tract, smooth muscle squeezes the food in our stomach and then pushes it through our intestines as it is digested. Smooth muscle is found in blood vessels, in the urinary tract, and in the air passages in the lungs. Smooth muscle is not under our direct control, and is sometimes referred to as *involuntary muscle*. Under the microscope, smooth muscle is not striped, and the muscle cells are woven and crisscrossed, not lined up in neat rows.

The third type of smooth muscle is *cardiac muscle*. It is found only in the walls of the heart. This type of muscle is also an involuntary muscle. That is good, for if we had to remember to tell our heart to beat, we wouldn't have time to think about anything else, much less sleep! Under the microscope, cardiac muscle cells look striped, like skeletal muscles, but they are arranged differently.

Connective tissue helps provide a framework for the body. It also helps connect and support other organs in the body. Connective tissue helps insulate the body, and it even helps transport substances throughout the body.

This tissue can be hard or soft. Some connective tissue stretches. One type is even fluid. If this seems like a riddle — after all, what kind of tissue could do and be *all* these things? — remember that "connective tissue" is a category that includes a lot of different tissues.

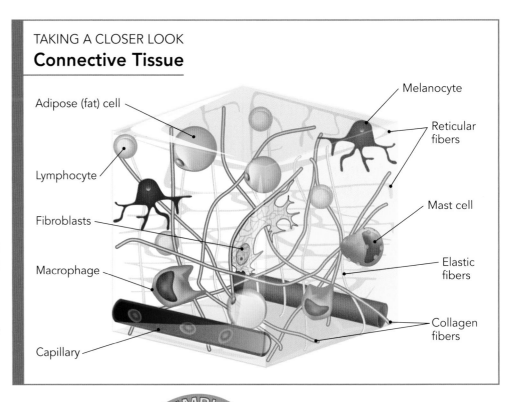

TAKING A CLOSER LOOK
Connective Tissue

Adipose (fat) cell

Lymphocyte

Fibroblasts

Macrophage

Capillary

Melanocyte

Reticular fibers

Mast cell

Elastic fibers

Collagen fibers

SO SIMPLE YET
Designed by the Master
SO COMPLEX

The Fibroblast

Connective tissue provides support and helps hold things together. These important functions would not be possible without a cell known as a *fibroblast*. The fibroblast is one of the most important cells found in connective tissue. The fibroblast is the cell most responsible for the production of *collagen fibers*. Collagen fibers help give connective tissue its strength. Fibroblasts also secrete the *ground substance* (or *matrix*) that fills in the space surrounding the fibers and cells of connective tissue. Fibroblasts also play a very important role in wound healing. When tissue is injured, fibroblasts migrate to the damaged area and help begin the healing process by making new collagen.

No wonder that fibroblasts are the one of the most common cells found in connective tissue. Without the fibroblast, we would fall apart!

There are many varieties of connective tissue. The fibrous capsules that cover many organs are connective tissue. The elastic fibers in the walls of arteries are connective tissue. The cartilage found throughout the body is connective tissue. Ligaments that bind bone to bone are connective tissue. Tendons that hook muscles to bones are connective tissue. Hard bone and soft *adipose* (fat) tissue are examples of connective tissue. Amazingly, even blood is considered connective tissue.

What do they all have in common? Well, for starters, connective tissues are each composed of three parts: cells, fibers, and ground substance.

Ground substance (also known as *matrix*) is the material that fills the space between the cells. It is composed mainly of fluids and protein.

The fibers of connective tissue are located in the ground substance. The most common type of fiber is made of long, stringy protein molecules called *collagen*. Collagen fibers are very tough and durable. They are coiled and intertwined and cross-linked to each other. In fact, ounce for ounce, a common type of collagen fiber is stronger than steel!

The cells must manufacture the fibers and the ground substance that make up connective tissue.

Without connective tissue we would fall apart.

Nervous tissue is the primary component of the nervous system. The nervous system regulates and controls bodily functions.

Nerve cells are called *neurons*. Neurons are able to receive signals from other cells, generate a signal, or *nerve impulse*, and transmit a signal to other nerve cells or organs.

Nervous tissue is found in the central nervous system and the peripheral nervous system. The central nervous system has only two parts: the brain and the spinal cord. The peripheral nervous system consists of all the other nerves outside your body; in other words, all the nervous tissue outside the brain and spinal cord.

TAKING A CLOSER LOOK
Types of Neurons

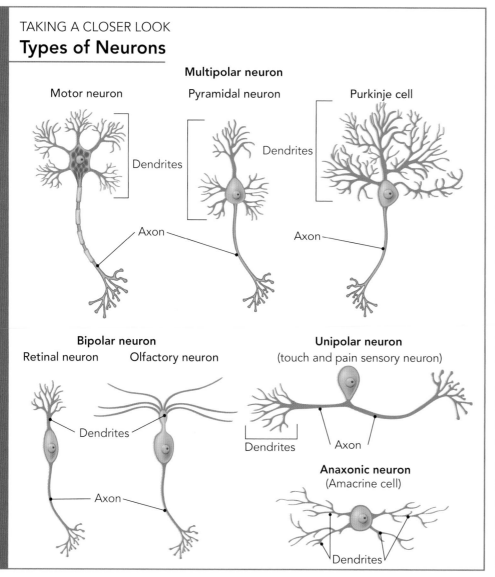

Multipolar neuron

Motor neuron   Pyramidal neuron   Purkinje cell

Dendrites

Dendrites

Axon   Axon

Bipolar neuron

Retinal neuron   Olfactory neuron

Unipolar neuron
(touch and pain sensory neuron)

Dendrites

Dendrites   Axon

Axon

Anaxonic neuron
(Amacrine cell)

Dendrites

4

ORGANS & ORGAN SYSTEMS

An organ is a collection of various types of tissues that work together to perform a function. The heart is an organ. The kidney is an organ. A lung is an organ. Each of these organs is designed to do certain things. The heart pumps blood, the kidney rids the body of waste products and extra water, and the lungs get oxygen into the blood and carbon dioxide out. Other organs are the brain, liver, stomach, gall bladder, small intestine, large intestine, pancreas, spleen . . . you get the idea.

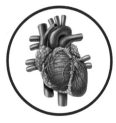
Heart

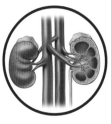
Kidney

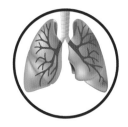
Lung

Brain

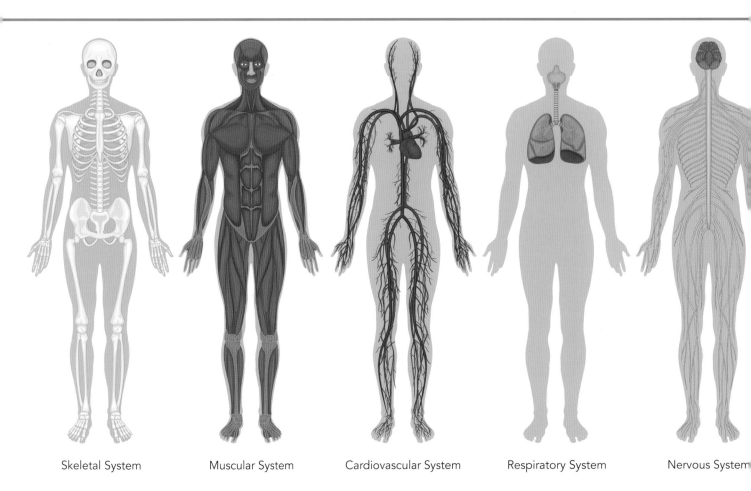

Skeletal System   Muscular System   Cardiovascular System   Respiratory System   Nervous System

However, even as important and complex as each organ is, none can do their job alone. They require other organs and structures to assist them. The heart cannot function without the veins and arteries. The kidney cannot function without the ureters and the bladder. The lungs would be useless without the nose, the trachea, and the bronchial tubes to bring air to them and the diaphragm to help the chest cavity to expand and draw air in. No part of the digestive tract would do you any good if the other parts weren't there for food to travel through as it gets digested.

These collections of organs and structures are called organ systems. The heart, veins, and arteries, for instance, are parts of the circulatory system. The kidneys, ureters (tubes that drain the kidneys), and the bladder are the urinary (or excretory) system. The lungs are part of the respiratory system. It is logical

Programmed Cell Death

Did you know that some cells are designed to self-destruct? This process is called *programmed cell death*. Our Creator designed this process to eliminate worn out cells, but that's not all! Programmed cell death also makes it possible to shape a developing baby's delicate body parts. For instance, long before birth, a baby's fingers are webbed. Once the fingers reach a certain stage of growth, the cells in the webs die away and leave the individual fingers. In an adult, programmed cell death serves to keep the right number of healthy cells in many tissues and organs so that they maintain the correct shape and don't grow too large. When a cell receives a self-destruct signal, enzymes that chop its largest molecules into pieces are activated. The cell shrinks, becomes a misshapen blob, and disintegrates.

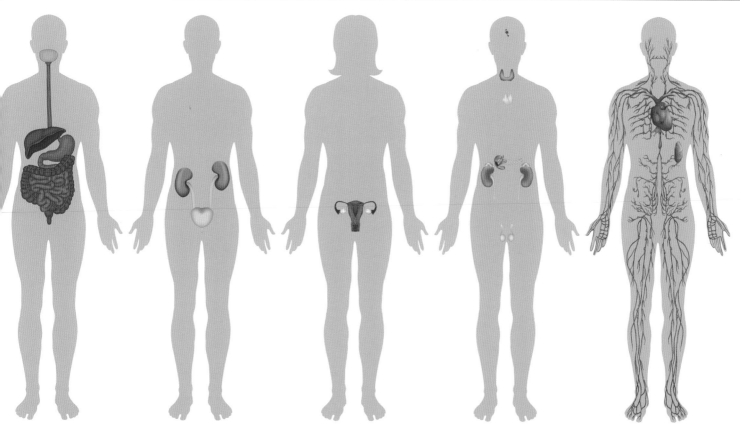

Digestive System   Urinary System   Reproductive (female) System   Endocrine (male) System   Lymphatic System

to explore the enormous complexity of the human body by breaking it down into the various organ systems.

Body System	Organs Included
Skeletal System	Bones and joints
Muscular System	Muscles
Cardiovascular System	Heart and blood vessels
Respiratory System	Upper airway (nose, pharynx, larynx), trachea, and lungs
Nervous System	Brain, spinal cord, and nerves
Digestive System	Mouth, esophagus, stomach, intestines, liver, gall bladder, and pancreas
Urinary System	Kidneys, ureters, and bladder
Reproductive System	(Male) Testes, genital ducts, and prostate (Female) Ovaries, uterus, fallopian tubes, and breasts
Integumentary System	Skin, nails, and hair
Endocrine System	Pituitary gland, hypothalamus, thyroid gland, parathyroid glands, pancreas, adrenal glands, testes (male), and ovaries (female)
Lymphatic System	Lymph nodes, lymph vessels, thymus, tonsils, and spleen

But They Are Not Really Separate

Even though we will be examining each organ system separately, they are not really separate or independent. Each one requires one or more of the others to function correctly.

For example, the bones in the skeleton cannot function without the vitamin D that is provided when the skin (integumentary system) produces vitamin D in response to sunshine. If the digestive system did not break down food to get energy, then no other system could operate. The same could be said of the circulatory system that provides oxygen to tissues and removes carbon dioxide. And, of course, the circulatory system could not deliver oxygen to the rest of the body if the respiratory system didn't bring oxygen into contact with blood pumped to the lungs by the heart. *Hormones* secreted by the endocrine system help regulate the action of the kidneys. The muscles in the legs (muscular system) compress

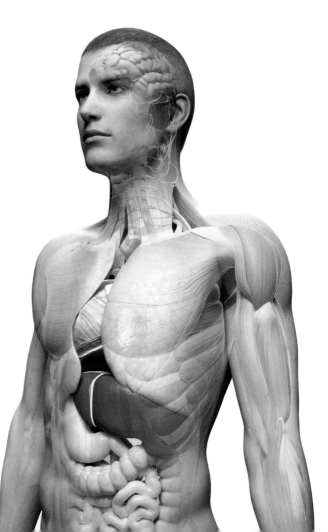

veins and help return blood to the heart (circulatory system). The list could go on and on.

Directions on the Map of Your Body

A very important aspect of the study of anatomy is knowing where certain things are in relation to other things. That being the case, there are special terms that anatomists use to help navigate around the body. This all begins with a reference point known as the *anatomical position*.

The anatomical position is defined as the body in an upright posture with the feet spread slightly apart. The arms are down to each side with the palms of the hands turned forward with the thumbs pointing away from the body. This is the starting point from which we describe where one part is in relation to another.

The most common terms used to describe the location or position of body parts are as follows:

Anterior and *posterior* — These describe structures at the front (anterior) or the back (posterior) of the body. If an organ is closer to the front of the body than another, it is said to be anterior to the other organ. Your belly button is anterior to your backbone.

Proximal and *distal* — These describe whether something is closer (proximal) or farther away (distal) from the middle of the body. For example, the knee is proximal to the foot, and the hand is distal to the elbow.

Medial and *lateral* — These describe whether something is closer (medial) or farther away (lateral) from the midline, or center line, of the body. For example, the ears are lateral to the eyes.

Superior and *inferior* — These describe whether something is above (superior) or below (inferior) something else. For example, the knee is inferior to the hip.

There are, of course, many other anatomic terms. We will occasionally be introducing these through this series.

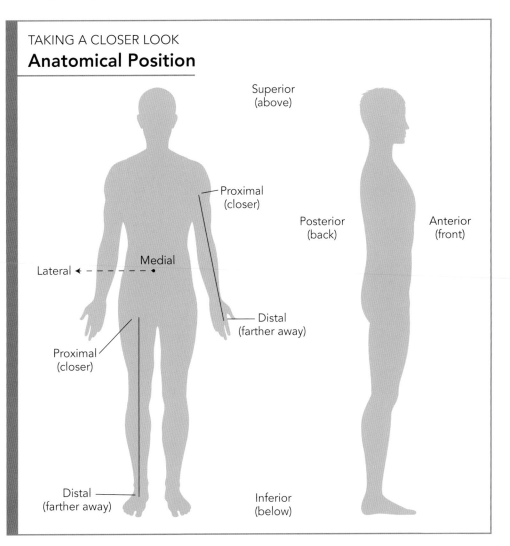

TAKING A CLOSER LOOK
Anatomical Position

Superior (above)

Proximal (closer)

Posterior (back)

Anterior (front)

Medial

Lateral

Distal (farther away)

Proximal (closer)

Distal (farther away)

Inferior (below)

5

HOMEOSTASIS

Before we proceed further there is a basic concept in physiology that you need to understand. That concept is called homeostasis. This means the body has many mechanisms to help maintain a balance or "equilibrium" among its many systems. The body functions best within certain limits. You need to have plenty of water in your body, but not too much. Body temperature can vary a little, but it normally stays not too high and not too low. The minerals in your body are very important, but it is also important that you have neither too much nor too little of them circulating in your bloodstream.

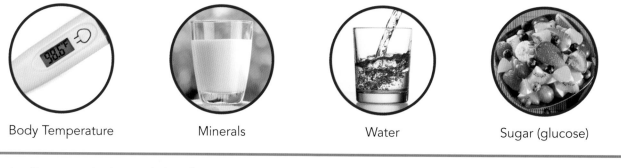

Body Temperature   Minerals   Water   Sugar (glucose)

An example of homeostasis: the regulation of blood sugar

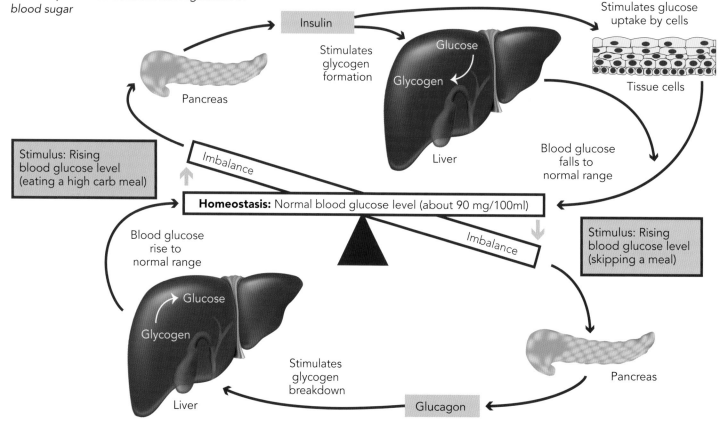

There are trillions of cells, multiple types of tissues, and many organs and organ systems in our bodies. All try to continue functioning as they were designed. All the cells, tissues, and organs must work together to achieve this goal.

However, the internal environment of the body must be kept within strict ranges in order for these systems to operate correctly. There are many, many control systems in our bodies designed to help maintain the necessary balance.

For example, our body temperature must be kept within a very narrow range. If our body temperature gets too high or too low, cells cannot work properly. You will see that there are control systems to monitor and help maintain correct body temperature.

The amount of sugar in our blood must be kept within certain limits. You will see that multiple systems play a role in controlling our blood sugar. The same could be said about the amount of calcium or potassium in our blood, the volume of fluid in our blood vessels, or the level of acids in our body.

Even though the human body contains countless little factories in about a dozen organ systems working simultaneously day and night, drawing on resources and producing waste products like acids, carbon dioxide, and excess heat, the human body is designed to maintain homeostasis, a constant set of conditions under which all the tissues work best. We will examine many of the feedback systems that help achieve this balance, and we will also see instances of what happens when things go wrong.

SO SIMPLE YET
Designed by the Master
SO COMPLEX

Is It All an Accident?

The number of intricate relationships that exist between organ systems is truly mind-boggling. Amazingly, many people think that all these organs and systems and the manner in which they interact is merely a cosmic accident, a product of time and chance. They attribute all this to chemicals banging together over millions of years. Their view is that given enough time, anything can happen.

As we proceed, it will be apparent that the human body is not just an accident. Nothing this complex can happen by chance. Many of the body's systems cannot work unless others are already in place and working properly. This "irreducible complexity" leaves no wiggle room for the random processes of evolution. There is a design and a purpose to how the body works. We are truly "fearfully and wonderfully made." The human body is a testament to the power and majesty of our Creator God.

THE SKELETAL SYSTEM

Just as a house needs a solid foundation, so it must have a strong framework to support it. Wooden or metal beams are connected by structural steel to form the skeletal structure of the home. All this is done before the brick or other siding covers the outside, and wood, plaster, or other materials cover the inside walls. God created us with a brilliantly designed skeleton that can move with us, support us, and help get us wherever we need to go!

Thousands of years ago, there was much misunderstanding about the human body and how everything worked together so intricately. However, God has always known, and those who followed Him gained insights into the mastery of the Creator. It was God who called forth light from the vast darkness. It was also God who intricately formed Adam from the dust. The brilliant arrangement of the human body was not lost on the prophet Ezekiel when he had a vision of dry bones in a valley:

The hand of the Lord came upon me and brought me out in the Spirit of the Lord, and set me down in the midst of the valley; and it was full of bones... And He said to me, "Son of man, can these bones live?" So I answered, "O Lord God, You know." Again He said to me, "Prophesy to these bones..." So I prophesied as I was commanded; and as I prophesied, there was a noise, and suddenly a rattling; and the bones came together, bone to bone. Indeed, as I looked, the sinews and the flesh came upon them, and the skin covered them over; but there was no breath in them (Ezekiel 37:1-8).

Both giraffes and humans have seven bones in their necks.

The vertebral column is made up of 26 bones.

Your bones are about six times stronger than steel, if measured by weight.

Bone marrow helps to create red and white blood cells, and these help us in many ways, including fighting bacterial infections.

FUNCTIONS OF THE SKELETAL SYSTEM

The most recognizable organ system in the human body is probably the skeletal system. Skeletons are popular props in movies, and most people have seen a picture of one or even a plastic or cardboard model of a human skeleton somewhere. But as important as all those big bones are, the skeletal system contains many small, less familiar bones as well as the ligaments that hold the bones together, the cartilage that cushions many of their ends, and the joints that allow them to move with stability and purpose.

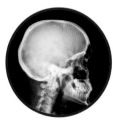

Skull

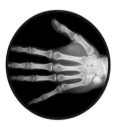

Hand

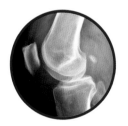

Knee Joint

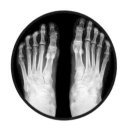

Feet

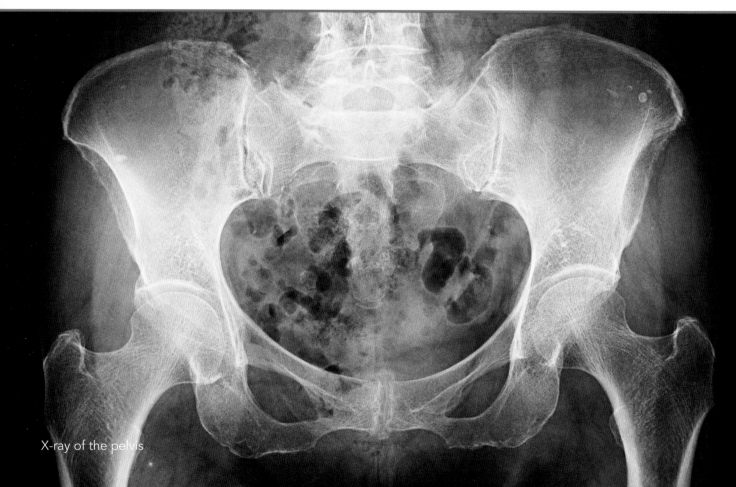

X-ray of the pelvis

Bones make up about 20 percent of the mass of the body (say about 30 pounds in a 150-pound person), and they consist mostly of connective tissues. And while bones obviously hold you up, they actually do a lot of other less dramatic but equally important things.

The first, and most obvious, function of the skeletal system is indeed to provide *support* for the body — to hold you up. We could not stand up, move around, pick things up, or even breathe properly if not for the framework of the skeleton. The bones provide a structure to bear weight so we can walk. They provide attachments for the muscles to help keep us upright. Without the bones inside us, we would all be just big lumps of tissue lying on the ground!

The second function of the skeletal system is to provide *protection* for our other organ systems. The skull protects the brain. Without the skull's cranial cavity to cradle your brain, it could be damaged by simply combing your hair or laying your head on your pillow, and bumping your head would be disastrous.

The rib cage is a protective shield for the heart and lungs and provides a sturdy space into which your lungs can expand. God designed your bones to protect these three very important organs as well as many other less obvious ones. The strength of the bones themselves help keep muscles, blood vessels, and several abdominal organs from being crushed when we fall or are struck by some object.

The bones of the skeleton do not move themselves, but without them we could not move. Why? Because the bones provide places where muscles can attach. The muscles then contract, and bones to which they are attached move. Bend your knee. A muscle behind your thigh pulled on a bone below your knee. Make a fist. Several muscles in your forearm pulled on the bones in your fingers. You get the idea!

The skeletal system is also a great warehouse for storing many things the body uses regularly. Bones can store certain types of fats that the body needs to hang onto. Bones also store certain minerals, such as calcium, magnesium, and phosphate. These minerals are constantly needed by the body, and it is important that the body have a reservoir of them to draw on so that the amounts of these minerals in the blood can be kept at a safe and fairly constant level. As the body uses these minerals, their concentration in the blood decreases. When this decrease is detected, the minerals stored in the bones are released to return the mineral levels in the blood to normal. At the same time, the mineral stores in the bones are resupplied from the minerals we take in from our diet.

Finally, your bones are where most of your *blood cells* are made! Most of our blood cells are formed (by a process called *hematopoiesis*) in the marrow cavities of the many bones of the body. We would be in quite a fix without a constant resupply of blood.

Blood cells die rapidly. Some blood cells live for only a matter of days. Some can live a few months. When they die, they need to be replaced. If we could not constantly make new blood cells, we could not survive.

So you can see our bones do more than just hold us up. They do much more!

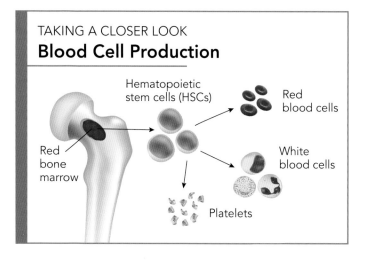

TAKING A CLOSER LOOK
Blood Cell Production

Hematopoietic stem cells (HSCs)

Red bone marrow

Red blood cells

White blood cells

Platelets

2

BONES

If you have ever spent time looking at a skeleton, you will see that bones come in many shapes and sizes. Anatomists have sorted bones into certain classes based on their shape.

Long Bones   Short Bones   Flat Bones   Irregular Bones

Major Bones in the Body

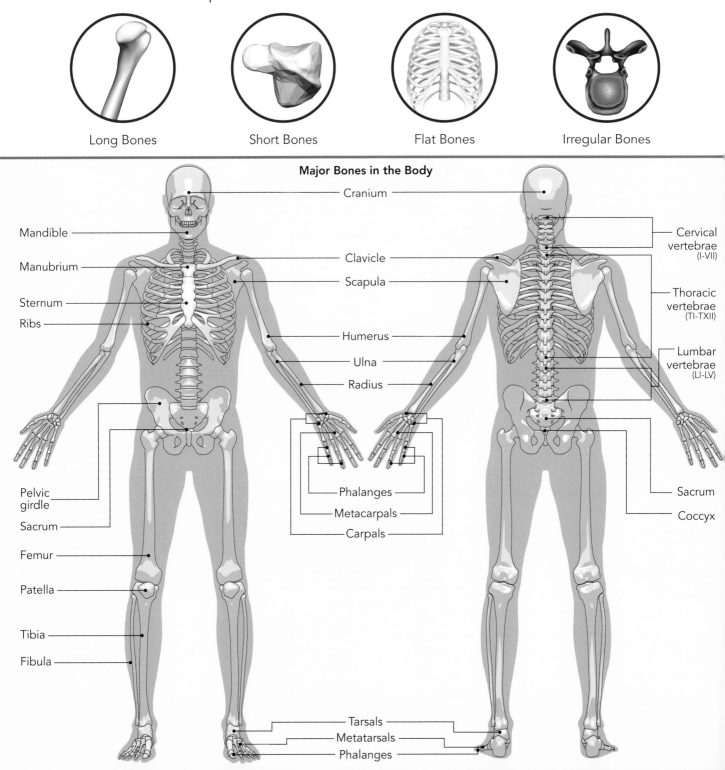

Cranium

Mandible

Manubrium

Sternum

Ribs

Clavicle

Scapula

Humerus

Ulna

Radius

Cervical vertebrae (I-VII)

Thoracic vertebrae (TI-TXII)

Lumbar vertebrae (LI-LV)

Pelvic girdle

Sacrum

Femur

Patella

Tibia

Fibula

Phalanges

Metacarpals

Carpals

Sacrum

Coccyx

Tarsals

Metatarsals

Phalanges

First, there are the *long bones*. These bones are longer than they are wide. Examples of long bones are the humerus (the upper arm), the femur (thigh bone), and the tibia (the shin bone). Look at the picture of the skeleton. Find these bones and see if you can pick out some other long bones.

When you looked at the skeleton to find the long bones, you probably saw the other bone in the lower leg (the fibula) and the two bones in the forearm (the radius and the ulna) right away. (By the way, the end of the ulna is what you hit when you hit your "funny bone." The radius is the forearm bone nearest your thumb.) Did you find some smaller long bones? Even though they are not that long, the bones in the fingers are considered long bones! They are longer than they are wide.

Short bones are, incredibly enough, called *short bones*. These are bones that are about as wide as they are long. The small bones in the wrist, called carpal bones, are short bones.

Bones that are thin are called *flat bones*. These bones can be either long or short, and they are usually curved. The bones in the skull are flat bones, as are the ribs. The skull's flat bones are fused together.

Bones that are small and round are called *sesamoid bones*. These bones are embedded inside tendons, and are found where tendons pass over joints. The most prominent sesamoid bone is your kneecap. Smaller sesamoid bones are found in the hands and feet.

Bones that cannot be easily placed in any of the categories

are called *irregular bones*. The bones in the vertebral column (backbone) are irregular bones.

Gross Anatomy of Bone

Gross anatomy examines the body at a macroscopic level. Let's examine the structure of a typical long bone from the outside in.

Remember, long bones are longer than they are wide. They are comprised of the diaphysis, the epiphyses, and the periosteum.

The main shaft or midsection of the bone is known as the *diaphysis* (don't let these terms spook you, you'll have them down in no time). It is made up primarily of thick *compact bone* and has a central cavity, called the *medullary cavity*. ("Medullary" means "in the middle.") Blood cell-making bone marrow or fat is stored in the medullary cavity of long bones.

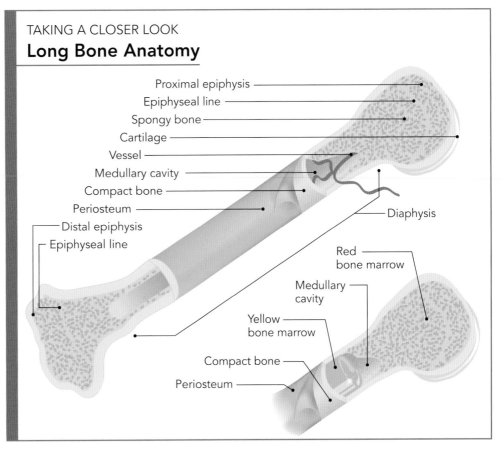

TAKING A CLOSER LOOK
Long Bone Anatomy

Proximal epiphysis
Epiphyseal line
Spongy bone
Cartilage
Vessel
Medullary cavity
Compact bone
Periosteum
Distal epiphysis
Epiphyseal line
Diaphysis
Red bone marrow
Medullary cavity
Yellow bone marrow
Compact bone
Periosteum

The rounded, broader end of a long bone (the joint end) is called the *epiphysis*. Joint surfaces are covered with a layer of cartilage, which makes the joints move smoothly. The joint cartilage also absorbs shock and cushions the joint during movement.

Now let's look more closely. . . .

The outermost layer of bone is a thin, fibrous membrane called the *periosteum*. It is a tough, durable structure that covers most of the outer surface (all except the joint surfaces) of all bones. The periosteum contains special nerve endings that sense pain, which is no surprise at all to anyone who has had a broken bone! Man, does THAT hurt! The periosteum also has blood vessels that help provide nutrients to the bone.

That seems quite a lot for a little membrane, but there's more. There are special cells in the periosteum that build new bone. These cells are very important as bone grows or when a bone is broken. We will see how later.

Finally, the periosteum helps provide a place for the tendons of muscles to attach to bones. Without those attachments, we would not be able to move!

Now let's look at the inner structure of a long bone.

If a bone is cut in cross section (see below), you can see that beneath the periosteum is a dense, thick layer that is called *compact bone*. As you might expect, compact bone is very durable and strong. It is primarily responsible for the support of the body. Because it is so dense, between 75 and 80 percent of the weight of the skeleton is due to compact bone.

The innermost part of the bone is not as dense. It is almost like a sponge or a honeycomb in its

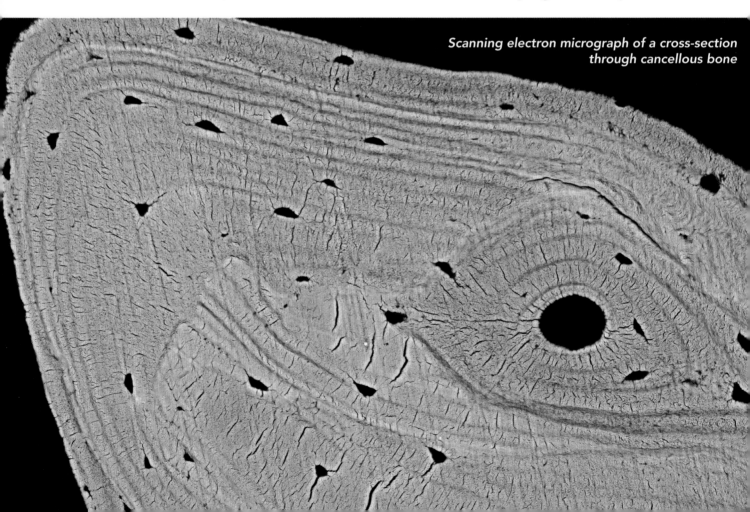

Scanning electron micrograph of a cross-section through cancellous bone

Tips for Healthy Bone

There are steps you can take to keep your bones healthy!

Your bones must get the calcium and phosphorus they need from your diet. Phosphorus is plentiful in most foods, so it is unusual to run low on this mineral. However, it is important to make sure you eat and drink plenty of calcium. Good sources of calcium are milk, dairy products, and leafy green vegetables. The more, the better!

Also, getting enough sunlight (but don't get sunburned!) is important. You see, when our skin is exposed to sunlight, vitamin D is produced. Vitamin D helps your intestines take in calcium from the food you eat.

Another thing that keeps bones healthy is exercise. The stresses that are placed on bones as you run or play sports, lift weights, walk, or run help keep them strong. Because your bones are designed to detect how strong they need to be, weight-bearing exercise (like running, but not swimming) actually cause the osteoblasts to make your bones stronger.

appearance. In fact, it is often referred to as *spongy bone*. (It is also called *cancellous bone*.)

In a typical long bone, the spongy bone is found primarily near the ends of the bones, close to the joints. In the center of the diaphysis (remember, the mid shaft of a long bone), is found the medullary cavity. This cavity contains either red bone marrow, where blood cells are made, or yellow bone marrow, where fats are stored.

What Goes On Inside

The inside of a bone is actually a very busy place. However, looks can be deceiving. Bones are one of the most active organs in the body.

They are constantly building and rebuilding, not only to grow or repair injuries, but even to remodel themselves in response to the stresses our activities put on them. And for the most part, that stress is actually *good* for our bones. Why? Because bones respond to this by becoming even stronger.

Bones also respond to signals from other parts of the body. For instance, the bones are the warehouses from which important minerals like calcium or phosphorous can be quickly accessed and released. And as key blood-making centers, bones rapidly respond to infection or blood loss by producing more of the right kinds of blood cells.

In order to truly understand how amazing bones are, we need to take a much closer look. We will start with three tiny cells . . . three kinds of bone cells.

Bone Cells

Bone activity is controlled primarily by the actions of three different cell types: the osteoblast, the osteoclast, and the osteocyte. These all sound very much alike, and there is a reason for this. All three names begin with the prefix "osteo," which is the Greek word for "bone." (Clever, huh?)

The term "cyte" means cell. "Blast" means "immature or precursor." "Clast" means "something that breaks." You can now guess what each cell does.

An *osteocyte* is a mature bone cell. An *osteoblast* is an immature cell or a bone-building cell. *Osteoclasts* break down bone. Thanks to the combined actions of these cells, bone is like a construction zone in which the project is never finished.

Building Bone — Osteoblast

The function of the osteoblast is simple: it builds new bone. Whether in a bone that is getting bigger as a person gets older, a bone that is healing after a fracture, or simply a bone that is being remodeled, the osteoblast has a vital role.

Remember that bone is a connective tissue. One characteristic of connective tissue is that it has ground substance (also called *matrix*). The osteoblast makes the ground substance in bone. The bony matrix consists of collagen protein fibers made strong by minerals that are added to them.

The osteoblasts make collagen, a strong fibrous protein. The long collagen fibers are laid down outside the osteoblast cells. Collagen gives bone its *tensile strength*. (That just means "strength under tension.") It keeps bone from pulling apart and makes it somewhat flexible.

After making the collagen fibers, the osteoblasts deposit mineral salts on them. Those mineral salts contain calcium and phosphorus. Mineralization makes the bones strong and hard.

Resorbing Bone — Osteoclast

The osteoclast is a cell that resorbs or breaks down bone. This might seem odd that there is a cell that breaks down bone. After all, aren't bones better if they are stronger? Why would a cell take away bone? Well, there is a good reason for this.

As has been mentioned, bone is a very dynamic tissue. You will see this in how bone constantly remodels itself. When bone wears out, the osteoclasts help remove it so it can be rebuilt.

Osteoclasts are large cells with multiple nuclei. When seen under the microscope, the osteoclast is often said to look "foamy." This is because the

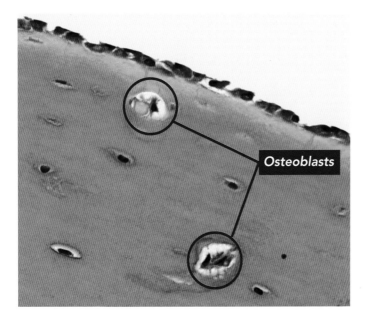
Osteoblasts

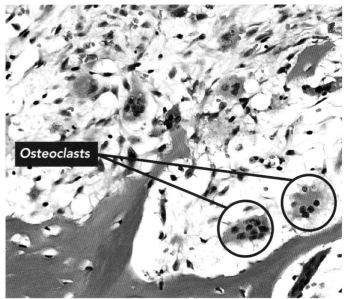
Osteoclasts

cytoplasm of the osteoclast contains lots of vesicles containing the substances needed to help break down bone tissue.

Mature Bone — Osteocyte

When osteoblasts become trapped in the ground substance, they become osteocytes. Osteocytes are mature bone cells that have become walled off within the bone they have made.

In compact bone, osteocytes are located in spaces called lacunae. These cells have long extensions, called "processes" (sometimes called "legs"), that reach through small channels in the bone and come in contact with processes from other osteocytes. In this way, even though they are walled off from other cells, the osteocytes can communicate with one another.

There was a time when osteocytes were thought to have little function, but it is now known that these cells are more than just inactive osteoblasts. Osteocytes can act as sensory cells that help control the activity of osteoblasts and osteocytes. They can help detect how strong your bones need to be and let the other cells know. Through contact with other osteocytes via these "processes" they can transmit signals to other cells.

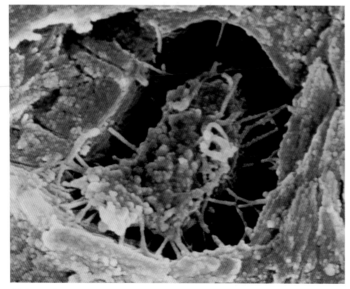

Osteocyte

Bone Structure

Let's take a look at how bones work. We will start with compact bone.

The basic unit of compact bone is called an *osteon*. An osteon looks like a long tube or cylinder made up of layers. These layers are called *lamellae*. In the center is a canal that contains blood vessels and nerve fibers. (You might not think so by its external appearance, but bone has a very rich blood supply.) Surrounding this central canal are layers of ground substance. Between the lamellae are found the small chambers, or *lacunae*, where the osteocytes are found. The processes of the osteocytes extend through the lamellae to communicate with other bone cells.

One way to visualize the osteon is to think of the rings in a tree trunk. The rings get bigger as you go out from the center. So it is with the layers of the osteon: they get larger as you move from the center.

Multiple osteons are packed together with extra ground substance to hold them together. This extra material can be thought of as glue that holds the osteons in place.

The outer layer of compact bone is made up of very large rings of ground substance and osteocytes. These rings are called *circumferential lamellae*, because they encase all the osteons in the circumference of the bone. The fibrous outer covering of the bone, the periosteum, covers the circumferential lamellae.

Spongy bone is somewhat different from compact bone in that it is not packed as tightly in appearance. It looks much like a sponge, and at first glance it seems quite random in its layout. However, our Master Designer is not that haphazard in His design. As it turns out, the struts of spongy bone are laid out precisely to manage the weight and stress placed on our bones! It's not random at all.

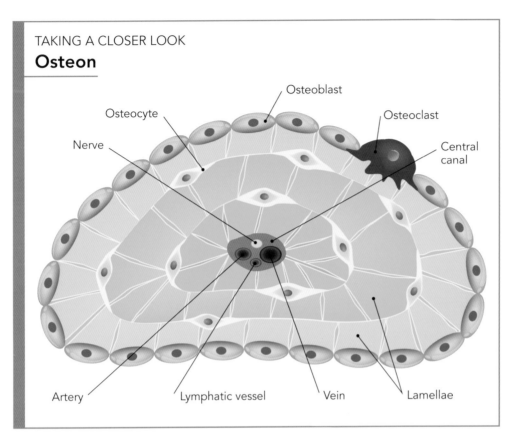

TAKING A CLOSER LOOK
Osteon

Osteoblast

Osteocyte

Osteoclast

Nerve

Central canal

Artery

Lymphatic vessel

Vein

Lamellae

When you examine spongy bones you will see the struts, called *trabeculae*, most prominently. Under a microscope, you will not see osteons in spongy bone like in compact bone. Rather, you will note that the trabeculae are made up of irregularly shaped layers of bone. These are most commonly only a few layers thick. There are osteocytes in these layers.

In spongy bone, blood vessels are not found in the layers. Rather, the blood supply is located in the spaces between the trabeculae. (These spaces look like the air spaces in a sponge.)

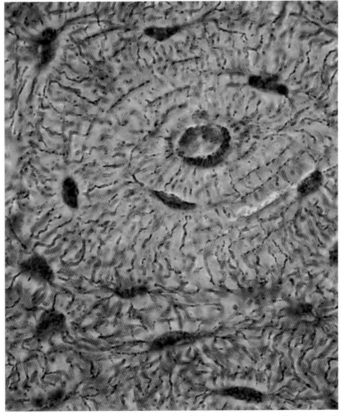

This is an osteon as seen through a light microscope. Compare it to the diagram above. Can you find the central canal surrounded by lamellae? How many osteocytes do you see?

Bone Growth

As we grow, our bones must grow also. This seems obvious, right? After all, we have very small twig-like leg bones as a newborn baby, but we have large strong leg bones as a teenager or adult. Our skeleton must grow along with the rest of our body.

Let's take a look at how this happens.

Bones do not grow by merely adding new bone tissue at the end. As it happens, bones could not grow like that. You see, most bones have joint surfaces at each end. A joint surface is covered by a layer of cartilage, which is a special type of connective tissue that helps protect the joint from stress and allows the joint to move smoothly. So obviously, bones cannot grow by putting new bone at the ends.

How bones grow is another testament to our wonderful Designer who created a special process by which bones can grow. Bones grow at an area called the *epiphyseal plate* (sometimes known as the growth plate).

Recall that a long bone has a main shaft (diaphysis) and rounded ends (each called an epiphysis). At the junction between the main shaft and a rounded end is a thin *epiphyseal plate* made of cartilage. On an X-ray, this plate looks like a gap in the bone. Growth of a long bone happens at the epiphyseal plate.

This is how a long bone grows longer. Cartilage is made by cells called *chondrocytes*, so there are chondrocytes in the thin cartilage of the epiphyseal plate. Along the side of the epiphyseal plate that faces the epiphysis, chondrocytes make new cartilage. However, the cartilaginous plate doesn't get thicker. Instead of the plate getting bigger, something interesting happens.

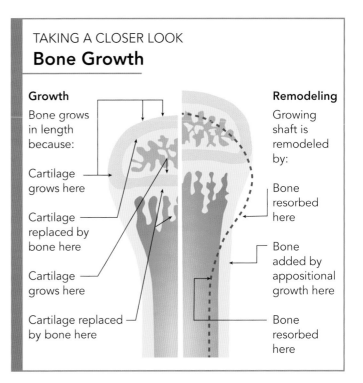

TAKING A CLOSER LOOK
Bone Growth

Growth

Bone grows in length because:

Cartilage grows here

Cartilage replaced by bone here

Cartilage grows here

Cartilage replaced by bone here

Remodeling

Growing shaft is remodeled by:

Bone resorbed here

Bone added by appositional growth here

Bone resorbed here

Growth Hormone

Human growth hormone (hGH) helps regulate bone growth. If a child's pituitary gland secretes too much hGH, *gigantism* can result, leading to a height of seven to nine feet! If the pituitary secretes too little hGH, the child is shorter than normal.

After the epiphyseal plates calcify with adulthood, bones cannot grow longer. Therefore excessive hGH in an adult causes bones in the hands, feet, and jaw to enlarge. This is called *acromegaly*.

Along the other side of the epiphyseal plate — the side next to the diaphysis — the chondrocytes die. The cartilage in this area of the plate begins to accumulate calcium. Then osteoblasts begin to make new bone there.

So, as the epiphyseal cartilage grows on the side of the epiphysis, new bone is formed on the side of the diaphysis. This is how the diaphysis (the main shaft of the bone) gets longer without disturbing the joint surfaces at the rounded ends.

If long bones did not grow like this, the joints would have to stop working while growing. Aren't you glad God designed your bones to grow longer from the epiphyseal plates so you can keep moving while your bones grow!

Ok, so that's how bones get longer, but don't bones get BIGGER? Yes, they do. They must, in order to withstand your weight as you grow. The long bones in a tiny baby are like little twigs and could never carry your weight. A long, very thin bone isn't of much use, is it?

Remember, we mentioned the membrane that covers the bone? That membrane is called the *periosteum*. Well, there are osteoblasts along the inner surface of the periosteum, and these cells make new bone. In this way the bone becomes thicker. But that can be a problem. When more bone is made it becomes heavier. It does not necessarily become stronger.

This process is kept under control by osteoclasts that are located in the middle (inside the medullary cavity) of the bone. The cells remove bone and make the medullary cavity bigger. In this fashion the bone gets larger but does not get too heavy.

Remember that all this activity is exquisitely regulated to keep too little bone from being made or too much bone from being broken down. Then end result is that we get bigger stronger bones.

Rickets

Rickets is a bone disease in children that is the result of a deficiency of vitamin D. The signs of rickets include bowed legs, defects in the spine or pelvis, and, on occasion, muscle weakness. Other signs include low blood calcium levels and an increased tendency for fractures.

The primary cause of rickets is a deficiency of vitamin D. Vitamin D aids in the absorption of calcium in the digestive tract. When vitamin D levels are low, less calcium is obtained from the diet. This lack of calcium leads to the skeletal defects characteristics of rickets.

The obvious treatment for rickets is to increase the levels of vitamin D. This can be accomplished by increased exposure to sunlight and increasing the intake of foods rich in vitamin D, such as eggs yolks and fish oils.

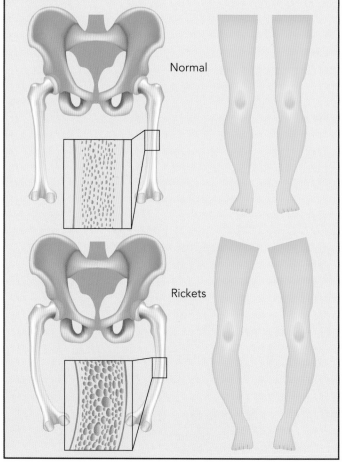

Normal

Rickets

The average person grows in height until around age 17 or 18. Due to hormonal changes, there is no significant change in height after that age. At that point, the epiphyseal plate becomes calcified, and is then called the epiphyseal line.

Bone Remodeling

Though bone does not look like it, it is, in fact, quite active even after a person has finished growing taller. Bone must continually build up and break down in order to remain healthy and strong. You see, as bone gets older, changes occur in the calcium compounds in the bone, causing the bones to become brittle. A brittle bone is more easily broken, so that could present a problem. Right? By getting rid of bone before it gets old and brittle and replacing it with fresh new bone, the bone stays strong and hard, yet just flexible enough to not be brittle.

God designed osteoclasts to break down and recycle older bone and osteoblasts to build new bone. We recycle about 5 percent of our bone mass every week!

In order to stay truly healthy, bones need to bear weight. Staying active therefore helps your bones remain strong. You have heard the phrase, "Use it or lose it!" People who exercise more tend to have stronger bones.

When weight is put on bones, they respond to this good kind of stress by making more bone tissue. Osteoblasts secrete more bony matrix when they are under stress. For example, football players who lift lots of weights have thicker bones at the points where the muscles attach to the bones. Tennis players tend to have stronger bones in their dominant arm. (Which arm depends on whether they are right or left handed.)

On the other hand, people who do not put much stress on their bones tend to have weaker bones.

For example, people who are sick and require long periods of bed rest lose bone strength. Astronauts who stay in space for long periods of time can also develop weaker bones, and therefore they must use special exercise equipment during long missions. These men and women have to exercise regularly; otherwise, the weightless environment in space would cause them to lose bone mass.

Bone and the Body

When we briefly described the various organ systems, it was said that even though each system could be

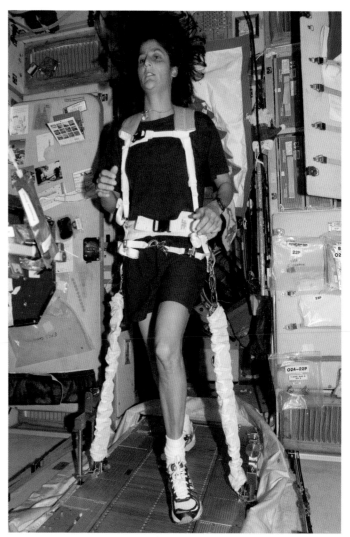

Without the stress of gravity during long missions in space, astronauts' bones lose calcium and strength without the proper exercise. Here astronaut Sunni Williams runs on the first treadmill installed on the International Space Station.

studied separately, they all truly work together. In this way, the entire body can function correctly.

It is important to remember this when we study the skeletal system. Our bones do so much more than just hold us up.

Let's look at one of the ways our bones interact with other systems in the body.

Bones store certain important materials that are needed for the body to function. One of the most important is calcium.

Calcium is obviously important to help us develop and maintain strong bones and teeth. In fact, about 98 percent of the body's supply of calcium is found in bones and teeth. But calcium is used for more than building bones and teeth. That other 2 percent is just as important. In fact, you couldn't live without it.

Calcium is vital for the operation of many other organ systems. Without calcium, blood could not clot, nerves could not transmit signals, muscles could not contract, and many enzymes could not work. *Enzymes* are special proteins that speed up and control chemical reactions in the body. So you see that calcium does more than make bones hard. It is needed in the proper concentration for many things.

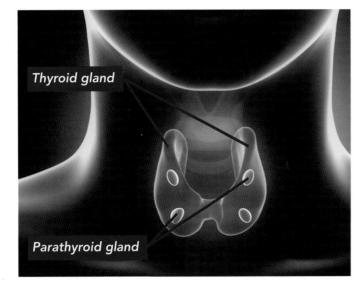

Thyroid gland

Parathyroid gland

Having either too much or too little calcium in the blood is dangerous.

So what does all this have to do with calcium being stored in bones? Well, our bones act as a sort of warehouse for calcium. When the body needs more calcium, it sends to the warehouse to get some more. How the body asks for more calcium is fascinating. It asks by using a hormone called PTH (parathyroid hormone). Hormones, remember, are chemical signals released from the brain or certain glands to tell other parts of the body what to do.

In our neck we have four small glands called parathyroid glands. These glands monitor the level of calcium in our blood. When the calcium level starts to get low, PTH is made and released into the blood. When PTH reaches the bones, osteoclasts are stimulated to act, and bone is broken down, releasing calcium into the blood. So, the calcium level in the blood goes up.

PTH can help increase the calcium level in other ways, too. PTH can signal the kidney to stop filtering out as much calcium. So if less calcium leaves the body in the urine, then more is kept in our blood. Another thing that PTH does is increase vitamin D production in the skin. Remember that vitamin D helps increase the amount of calcium we absorb from our food.

So when calcium levels go down, PTH production increases, and we get more calcium into our blood by extracting some from bone, absorbing more from our food, and losing less in our urine. Pretty neat, huh?

But are there times when the calcium level is too high? Yes, that does occur. Do we have a mechanism to correct this? Yes, we do!

There is another gland in our neck called the thyroid gland. It is a single gland, much larger than the parathyroids. The thyroid gland has several functions,

Osteoporosis

Osteoporosis is a disease, primarily of the elderly, that results in bones that are very fragile. It is a very serious health issue for older people in our society.

Osteoporosis occurs when bone *resorption* exceeds bone deposition. In other words, more of the bone gets broken down for recycling than gets replaced. This results in a loss of bone. Thus, the density of bone decreases over time. This decrease in bone density results is a much higher risk of fractures, particularly fractures of the spine or hip.

Osteoporosis is more common in women than in men. Risk factors for osteoporosis include a diet low in calcium, a history of smoking, and a lack of exercise.

The treatment of osteoporosis includes supplementation with calcium and vitamin D. In addition, patients can be given medications that decrease the activity of osteoclasts, which, in turn, slows the resorption of bone. An important part of both treatment and prevention of osteoporosis is weight-bearing exercise. Remember — putting stress on bones can be a good thing as it stimulates bones to build and become stronger.

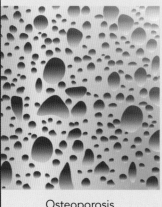

| Osteoporosis | Normal bone |

but among the hormones it makes is one called *calcitonin*. Do you notice part of the word "calcium" in the name "calcitonin"? Like the parathyroids, the thyroid gland monitors calcium blood levels. When the calcium level gets too high, calcitonin is secreted.

As you might expect, calcitonin does pretty much the opposite of PTH. Calcitonin decreases the activity of osteoclasts. Thus, less bone is broken down, and less calcium is released into the blood. Further, calcitonin decreases the amount of calcium absorbed from our food, and it stimulates the kidneys to release more calcium into the urine to be eliminated.

Thus, the blood level of calcium is maintained within very precise limits. Without types of monitoring systems such as this, our bodies would quickly be so out of balance that we could not function. This is an example of *homeostasis*, the body's way of keeping equilibrium in a system.

Arthritis

Arthritis is inflammation of one or more joints. Arthritis affects millions of people and is a leading cause of disability in people over the age of 65.

There are many kinds of arthritis. The most common are *osteoarthritis* and *rheumatoid arthritis*.

In osteoarthritis (OA), joint cartilage gradually deteriorates. This results in pain, swelling, and restricted motion in the joints affected. Aging, obesity, trauma, or overuse can cause osteoarthritis, especially in larger joints like knees and hips.

In rheumatoid arthritis (RA), a person's own immune system attacks the body's own tissues, often attacking the joints of smaller bones like those in the hands.

Broken Bones

Have you ever broken a bone? It wasn't very pleasant, was it? Sort of reminded you that we live in a fallen, sin-cursed world, right?

Obviously, a broken bone is not only very painful but it cannot function normally. You cannot walk properly on a broken ankle. If your arm is broken, you cannot throw a ball or lift a book. A break in a bone is called a *fracture*. We would be in quite a fix if broken bones stayed broken!

Fortunately, our Creator designed a way for fractured bones to heal and repair themselves. There are several stages to the healing process.

When a bone is broken, blood vessels inside the bone and in the periosteum are damaged. Blood leaks out of these damaged blood vessels. From this a mass of clotted blood called a *hematoma* forms at the place where the bone is broken.

Then, osteoblasts, along with two other types of connective tissue–producing cells, fibroblasts that make collagen and chondroblasts that produce

cartilage matrix, continue the healing process. A cartilage-like layer of tissue known as a *callus* is formed. The callus is made inside the fracture itself and also on the external surface of the bone. The callus provides support and helps stabilize the fracture as it heals.

Within a week or so, the callus made of cartilage begins to be converted to spongy bone. New trabeculae of spongy bone are made as healing continues. Over this period, the callus made of cartilage becomes a bony callus. Usually in six to eight weeks, the initial stages of healing are complete, and the bone is functional again.

But we are not done yet. As you recall, the outer part of bone is compact bone, not spongy bone. If the break in the bone were only filled in with spongy bone, the healed bone wouldn't be very strong, would it? Spongy bone is hard, but it isn't as hard by itself as it is when it is wrapped in compact bone. So something more must happen. After the fracture is initially healed with spongy bone, more bone remodeling is needed. Over the next 8 to 12 months, the bony callus undergoes a significant transformation. Osteoclasts begin the job of slowly breaking down the spongy bone. Then osteoblasts begin to make new compact bone to replace it.

TAKING A CLOSER LOOK
Repair of Broken Bones

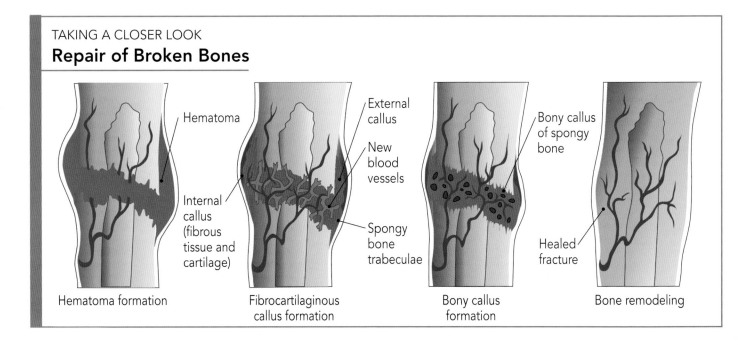

Hematoma — Internal callus (fibrous tissue and cartilage)

External callus — New blood vessels — Spongy bone trabeculae

Bony callus of spongy bone

Healed fracture

Hematoma formation

Fibrocartilaginous callus formation

Bony callus formation

Bone remodeling

The process of breaking down bone and making new bone has to be done in a very precise manner. There must be the proper balance at all times between removing old bone and making new bone.

After the bone remodeling at the fracture site is finished, there often remains a small thickening of the bone, a remnant of the callus left behind.

Types of Fractures

There are many different types of fractures that can occur. The simplest way of looking at these is to consider four basic categories: complete, incomplete, simple, and compound. Most fractures can be described using these categories.

Fractures may be *complete* or *incomplete*. A complete fracture is one where the bone breaks into two or more separate pieces. An *incomplete* fracture is one in which the bone is cracked but not broken all the way through.

A *simple fracture* (also called a *closed fracture*) is one in which the bone is broken but does not break though the skin. A *compound fracture* (also called an *open fracture*) is where the fractured bone breaks through the skin.

TAKING A CLOSER LOOK
Types of Fractures

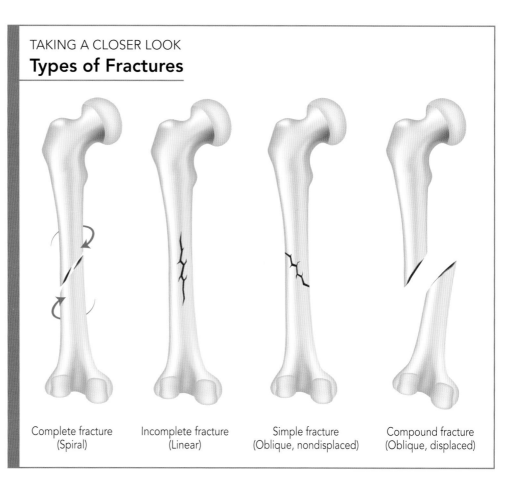

Complete fracture
(Spiral)

Incomplete fracture
(Linear)

Simple fracture
(Oblique, nondisplaced)

Compound fracture
(Oblique, displaced)

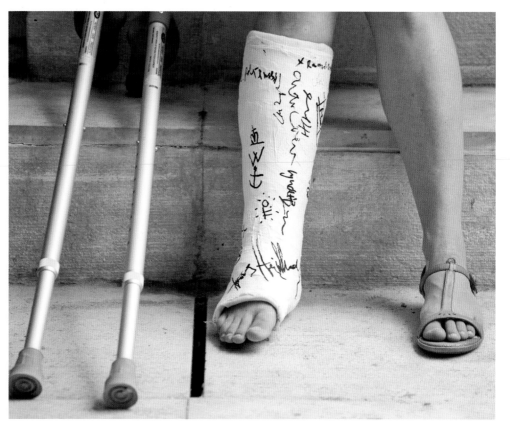

Replacing Joints

Joints severely damaged by arthritis or injuries can cause chronic pain and make it very difficult to move around. Sometimes these joints need to be surgically removed and replaced with an artificial joint made of metal, plastic, or ceramic. Hips and knees are the most commonly replaced joints. Hip replacement may be performed because of ongoing pain and decreased mobility, as in the case of arthritis, or in order to repair a broken hip.

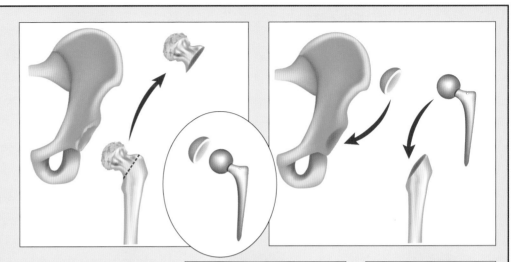

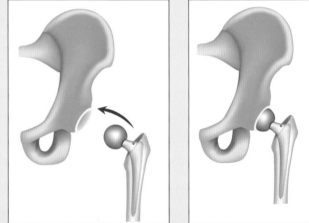

In a total hip replacement, pictured here, both the "ball" and the "socket" are being replaced. The head of the femur—the thigh bone—and the diseased cartilage that covers it are cut off. An artificial, or *prosthetic*, femoral head attached to a spike-shaped stem is inserted into the end of the femur. A cup-shaped ceramic socket is placed in the pelvic bone to cradle the new ball-shaped femoral head. During the healing process, a patient is given physical therapy to progressively increase the strength of the new joint and to encourage the patient to keep moving. With surgery like this, a person who was unable to walk or even get up out of a chair due to severe arthritis may be able to enjoy taking walks and moving more freely again.

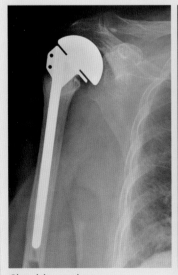

Shoulder replacement

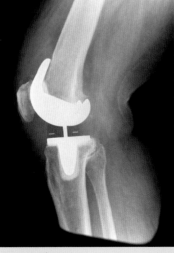

Knee replacement

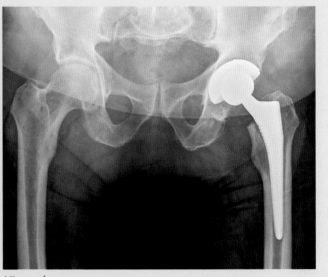

Hip replacement

Treatment of Fractures

A simple fracture is usually *immobilized* with a cast or a splint. This supports it while the healing process begins. By immobilizing the area so that the broken pieces of bone cannot shift, the cast can decrease the pain in the early days after a broken bone. Beyond this, a cast will help keep the person from putting weight or stress on the area before it can heal properly. And, of course, the better the fracture is immobilized, the less chance there is of disrupting the fragile material being laid down in the fracture site in the early stages of healing.

More serious fractures need more intensive intervention. Sometimes the bones are not in a proper position to heal correctly. In certain of these situations, the bones must be put into alignment. This is called a *reduction*. This can be very painful and often requires the patient be heavily sedated or even put to sleep for the procedure. After the proper position of the bones is achieved it can be put in a cast until it heals.

The most serious fractures sometimes require surgery. The surgeon may use nails, surgical screws, wires, plates, or rods to fix the bones into position to allow the fracture to heal. Surgical intervention for a fracture might be preferred over more conservative treatments in certain situations. For example, with hip fractures, surgery is the preferred treatment rather than having a patient endure a prolonged period of bed rest and immobilization.

Arthroscopy

To repair damaged joints, surgeons don't always have to make big incisions. Instead, joint damage sometimes can be repaired using arthroscopy. An arthrocope—a small telescope for looking into joints—is inserted through a small incision, usually only about an inch long. The joint can then be examined for any abnormality, such as torn ligaments or the effects of severe arthritis. Using other small instruments, a surgical repair can often be made with this technique.

Because the incisions are very small, the healing time for patients having arthroscopic surgery is much faster and they can soon return to their normal activities.

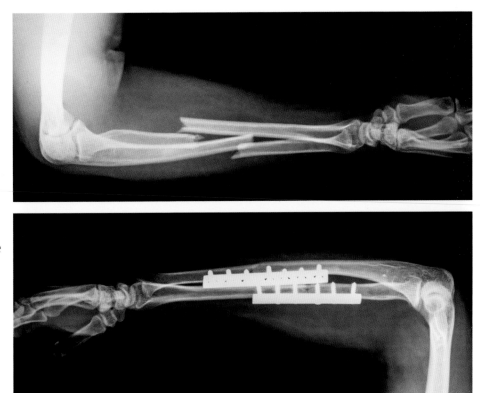

*This X-ray of the forearm shows a complete fracture of the **radius**, the bone behind the thumb, and the ulna, the bone beside it. The second X-ray taken after surgery shows that these bones have been realigned and plates attached to them to hold them in place for healing to occur.*

THE SKELETON

When people see a skeleton, the first thing many think of is something dead or something scary. In reality, nothing could be further from the truth.

The human skeleton is alive! It is composed of bones, ligaments that hold the bones together, cartilage, and joints. The skeleton is intricately designed but incredibly strong.

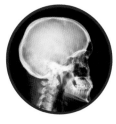
Skull

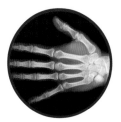
Hand

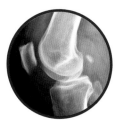
Knee Joint

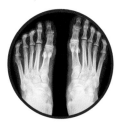
Feet

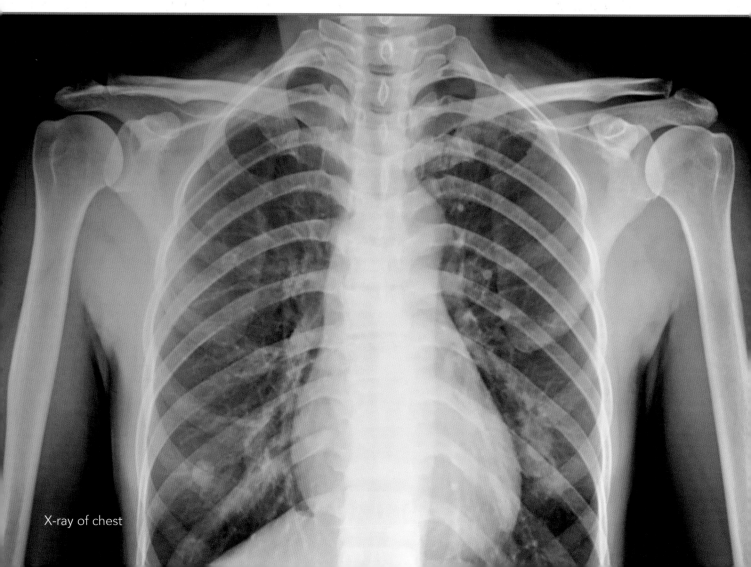
X-ray of chest

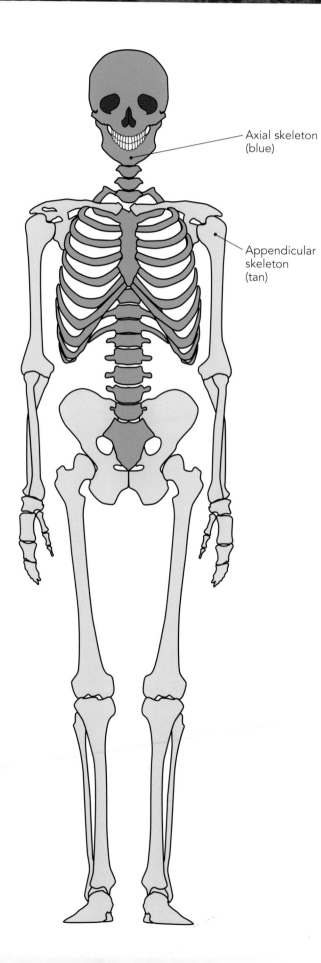

Axial skeleton
(blue)

Appendicular
skeleton
(tan)

The human skeleton of a newborn is made of 270 bones. As we grow and mature, some bones fuse together so that as adults we have a total of 206 bones. As we mentioned earlier, our skeletons account for about 20 percent of our body weight (say about 30 pounds in a 150-pound person).

The bones of the skeleton are divided into two groups, the *axial skeleton* and the *appendicular skeleton*.

The *axial skeleton* is made up of the skull, the vertebral column (the "back bones"), and the ribs. The skull protects the brain, gives us the solid foundation for a face, and holds our teeth so we can chew. The axial skeleton's vertebral column holds us upright so we can stand, walk, and sit without flopping over. The vertebral column protects the spinal cord, but is designed to allow us to bend and twist without damaging the delicate nerves on which all our voluntary movements depend. The ribs and vertebral column protect our heart and lungs and form a cavity into which the lungs can expand as we breathe.

The *appendicular skeleton* is made up of the upper and lower limbs as well as the bones that connect them to the axial skeleton. Without an appendicular skeleton we could not walk or run. We could not reach out and touch anything. We could not pick up or throw anything.

The arms are connected to the axial skeleton by the *pectoral girdle*. Your shoulder blades and collarbones are parts of your pectoral girdles. The legs are attached to the axial skeleton by the pelvic girdle. Your hipbones make up the *pelvic girdle*. The pelvis is like a bowl, open at the bottom, made of several hip bones fused together and attached to the lower part of the vertebral column.

Neither part of the skeleton is more or less important than the other. These divisions of the skeleton merely make it easier to systematically study and understand how the skeleton functions.

Terms of Movement

However, before we look at joints, we need to define anatomical terms of joint movement. That is, we need to understand the movement of joints themselves.

The most common joint movements are as follows:

Flexion and extension — Flexion means a movement that decreases the angle between two parts of the body. This is really not as complicated as it sounds. When you flex your elbow, you decrease the angle between the humerus and the ulna. When you flex your knee, you decrease the angle between the tibia and the femur. So logically, extension would be the opposite. Extension is where the angle between two parts of the body is increased. When you extend your elbow, the angle between the humerus and the ulna is increased.

Abduction and adduction — Abduction is movement away from the midline of the body. Adduction is movement toward the midline of the body. When you raise your arm directly away from your side, this is abduction of the shoulder joint. When you lower your arm back to your side, this is adduction of the shoulder.

Rotation — Rotation means moving a part around an axis. For example, when you turn your head from side to side, you are rotating the cervical vertebrae.

Other, more specific, anatomical movements will be defined later.

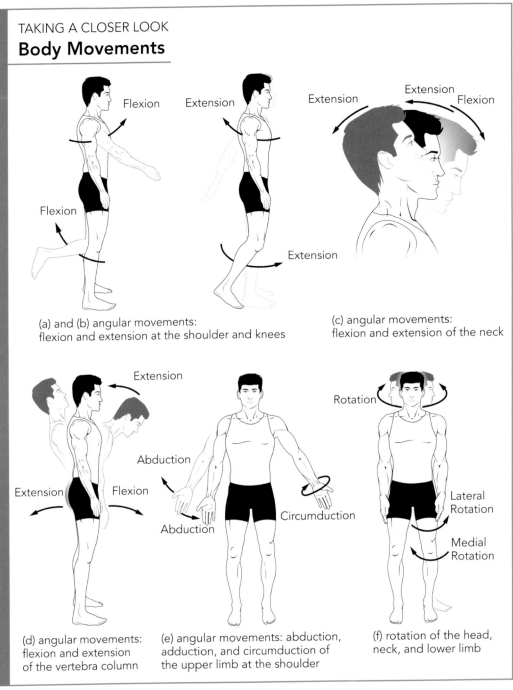

TAKING A CLOSER LOOK
Body Movements

(a) and (b) angular movements: flexion and extension at the shoulder and knees

(c) angular movements: flexion and extension of the neck

(d) angular movements: flexion and extension of the vertebra column

(e) angular movements: abduction, adduction, and circumduction of the upper limb at the shoulder

(f) rotation of the head, neck, and lower limb

Joints

Joints are the places where two or more bones meet, and they hold the skeleton together. Some joints allow a wide range of motion. Other joints allow for much less movement. Some joints allow no movement at all.

There are three categories of joints: *fibrous* joints, *cartilaginous* joints, and *synovial* joints.

Fibrous joints connect bones with dense fibrous connective tissue. Generally speaking, fibrous joints permit no movement. For example, the sutures between the bones of the skull are fibrous joints. In adults, these joints are immobile.

In *cartilaginous joints*, as you might have guessed, the bones are joined by cartilage. This type of joint allows very little movement. A *symphysis* is one place where bones are joined this way. The bones that form the front part of your pelvis are joined together at the *pubic symphysis*. The *pubic symphisis* is a cartilaginous joint.

The third type of joint, the *synovial joint*, allows the most movement. Most joints are synovial joints. When you think of a joint, you probably think of the synovial joints that allow you to move so well.

The ends of the bones in a synovial joint are covered by cartilage. Because the cartilage is inside a joint, it is called *articular cartilage*. (*Articulate* means

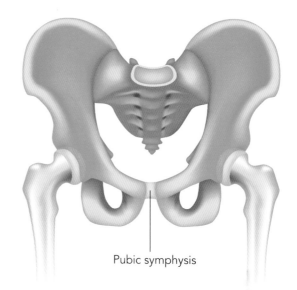

Pubic symphysis

"connected by a joint.") This cartilage provides a durable surface that allows the joint to move smoothly without damaging the bone underneath the cartilage. Imagine how uncomfortable it would be if the bare ends of the bones had to rub together, uncushioned by articular cartilage.

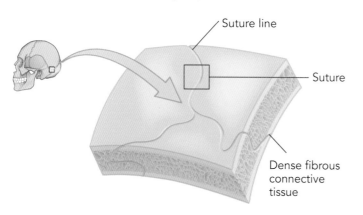

Suture line

Suture

Dense fibrous connective tissue

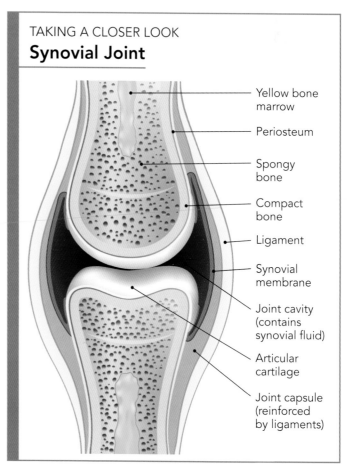

TAKING A CLOSER LOOK
Synovial Joint

Yellow bone marrow

Periosteum

Spongy bone

Compact bone

Ligament

Synovial membrane

Joint cavity (contains synovial fluid)

Articular cartilage

Joint capsule (reinforced by ligaments)

But the cartilage cushion alone isn't enough to make the synovial joints move freely. They need to be lubricated. The joint capsule makes such lubrication possible. The joint capsule has a tough fibrous layer on the outside and a lubricant-making layer called the *synovial membrane* on the inside. The outer dense connective tissue that surrounds the joint helps hold the bones together. The inner membrane is made of less dense connective tissue and helps create a space that contains a special fluid called *synovial fluid*. Synovial fluid lubricates the joint and reduces the friction produced when the cartilage covering the bone ends rub together. Beyond this, synovial fluid bathes the articular cartilage with oxygen and nutrients. This is very important, because there is no way for blood vessels to supply these things to the cartilage inside a moving joint, for they would be ripped and torn by the movement of the joint.

There are several types of synovial joints. Each makes a particular sort of movement possible.

First of all, there are *hinge joints*. You can think of this joint as being like a door hinge. This joint can flex or extend only. A hinge joint does not twist. The knee is an example of a hinge joint.

Saddle joints allow more motion than hinge joints. If a hinge joint can flex and extend in one plane, a saddle joint allows this flexion-and-extension, plus movement "side to side." The thumb joint is a good example. Try moving your thumbs up and down. Now move them side to side. You see, this range of motion is more complicated than a hinge joint. Just think of all the things you could not do if your thumb only moved in one plane!

A *ball-and-socket joint* is made of a rounded end of one bone fitting into a rounded cavity in another bone. This type of joint allows the maximum range of movement. It can move up and down, and side to side, as well as rotate. Your hip joint is a good example. Stop and see how many directions you can move your hip joint. Amazing, huh? This wide range of movement allows us to be able to run, walk, and change directions with ease. You have another ball-and-socket joint in your shoulder. Thus, you can raise and lower your arm, move your arm out from your side,

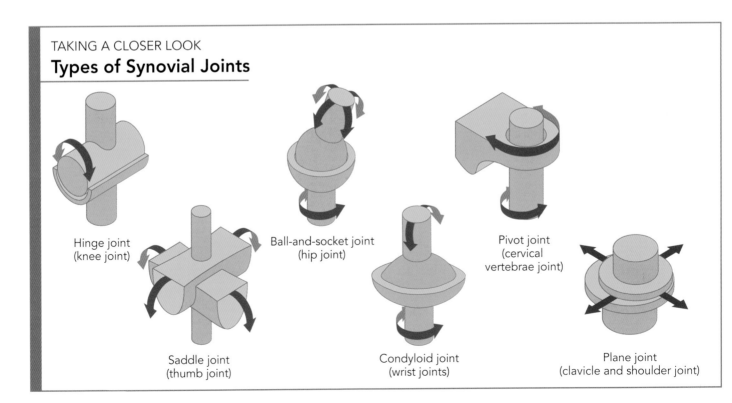

TAKING A CLOSER LOOK
Types of Synovial Joints

Hinge joint
(knee joint)

Ball-and-socket joint
(hip joint)

Pivot joint
(cervical
vertebrae joint)

Saddle joint
(thumb joint)

Condyloid joint
(wrist joints)

Plane joint
(clavicle and shoulder joint)

and rotate it 360 degrees. In fact, the joint around the shoulder is called the "rotator cuff" because rotation is such an important part of the shoulder's motions.

Condyloid joints are similar to ball-and-socket joints, but they are more restricted in the range of motion they allow. The joints in your wrist are condyloid joints.

A *pivot joint* is a relatively simple joint in that it primarily allows rotation. Think of turning your head, and you get the idea. The joint between the first and second cervical vertebrae is a pivot joint.

A *plane joint* is made up of flat surfaces and allows only a small gliding motion. The joint between the end of the clavicle and the shoulder blade, the acromioclavicular joint, is a plane joint. It allows just a little bit of movement.

Ligaments

You know, joints don't just stick together. If joints are to have the ability to move, then the surfaces of the joints must be able to glide or slide against one another. Ligaments make this possible.

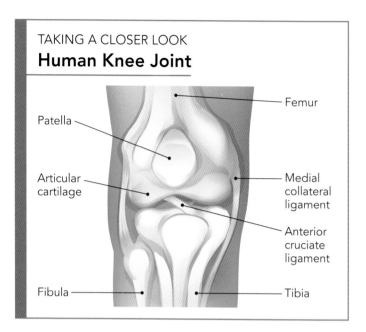

TAKING A CLOSER LOOK
Human Knee Joint

Patella

Articular cartilage

Fibula

Femur

Medial collateral ligament

Anterior cruciate ligament

Tibia

Ligaments are bands of dense fibrous connective tissue, primarily made of collagen fibers. They connect bone to bone to help form a joint. They are quite strong, but at the same time they are able to stretch to some degree and are, of course, very flexible. With movement of a joint, the ligament stretches. When the joint moves back, the tension is relieved and the ligament returns to its normal shape. In this way, ligaments help joints be stable while at the same time allowing joints their maximum range of movement.

Even though ligaments are strong and durable, they do have their limits. Perhaps you have heard about a football player who tore the ACL (anterior cruciate ligament) in his knee and had to have surgery to repair it. Or maybe you've heard about a pitcher in baseball who had to have surgery on his elbow to repair ligament damage. In cases like these, either through overuse or because of a sudden stress or impact, a ligament cannot withstand the force and is damaged.

Just as ligaments attach bones to other bones, so tendons are bands of connective tissue that attach muscles to bones. We'll learn more about them when we discuss muscles.

Gout

Gout refers to recurrent bouts of painful swelling and redness in a joint, often at the base of the big toe. Like other forms of inflammatory arthritis, gout can be quite debilitating.

Gout is caused by having elevated levels of uric acid in the blood. This uric acid can crystallize, and those tiny crystals can be deposited in the kidneys or in joints and tendons. Historically gout was thought to be a "rich man's disease" because it was more common in obese people who ate a lot of meat and consumed a lot of alcohol.

The Axial Skeleton

The axial skeleton is made up of the skull, the vertebral column, and the ribs. This division of the skeleton forms the central axis of the body. A very important function of the axial skeleton is that it protects the central nervous system (the brain and spinal cord) and the organs in the thorax (the heart and lungs). Eighty of the 206 bones in the body are in the axial skeleton.

The Skull

Perhaps the most recognizable part of the skeleton is the skull. The skull protects the brain. It has special cavities that protect our sense organs, without which we could not see, hear, smell, or taste. The skull contains the jaws and teeth that enable us to chew our food. It also is a place for our facial muscles to attach so we can smile, laugh, frown, grimace, and shape words with our mouths.

The Cranium

The most prominent feature of the skull is the cranium. This is the rounded part of the skull at the top. While it looks like one solid upside-down bowl, the cranium is actually made up of eight bones. In an adult, these bones are fused tightly together.

On the front of the cranium is the *frontal bone*. This is the bone in your forehead. Directly behind the frontal bone are the *parietal bones* (one on each side). If you touch the top of your head and run your fingers front to back, you will run your fingers

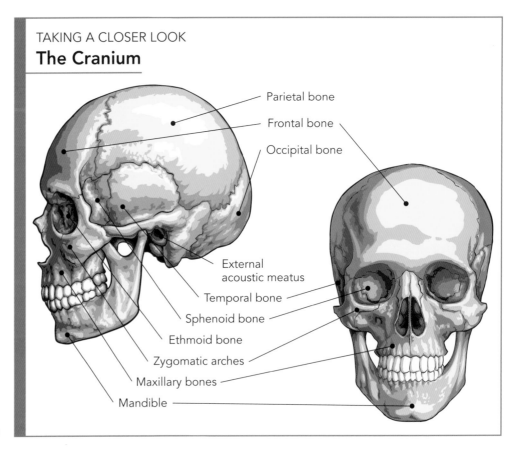

TAKING A CLOSER LOOK
The Cranium

- Parietal bone
- Frontal bone
- Occipital bone
- External acoustic meatus
- Temporal bone
- Sphenoid bone
- Ethmoid bone
- Zygomatic arches
- Maxillary bones
- Mandible

along the connection between your parietal bones. Lightly tap the bones on the top of your skull to each side. These are the parietal bones. Then on the *back* of your skull, protecting the part of your brain that enables you to see, is the *occipital bone*. (Your eyes are not on the back of your head, but they send information there!)

Looking from the side at a skull, you see one of the temporal bones. There is a *temporal bone* on each side, below the parietal bone. Your temples are named for your temporal bones. Buried within the thickest part of the temporal bone on each side is an intricately shaped labyrinthine chamber that perfectly matches the shape of your inner ear. In this little chamber, the delicate organs that enable you to keep your balance are protected. In front of the temporal bone is the *sphenoid bone*. The wing-shaped sphenoid bone forms a floor for your brain. Finally, located deep between the eyes is the *ethmoid bone*. The ethmoid bone has a lot of little holes through which the olfactory nerves pass to carry information about what you are smelling from your nose to your brain. The sinuses are formed by air cavities in some of these cranial bones.

Even though the cranial bones are fused together and therefore do not move in adults, they do have joints. The joints that hold the cranial bones together are called *sutures*. The word *suture* also means "stitch," so think of the fused cranial bones as being stitched together. These sutures are fibrous joints that hold bones together but permit no movement and so give our brains a great deal of protection.

The Facial Bones

The skull not only has cranial bones to protect the brain but also facial bones, including our jaws. The cheekbones you can feel below your eyes are called *zygomatic arches*. Below these are the *maxillary bones*. These form the upper jaw, and hold your upper teeth.

The most prominent of the facial bones is the *mandible*, or the lower jawbone. This is the only facial bone that moves. And it's a good thing it can. If the mandible could not move, we could not chew or speak.

Our lower teeth are anchored in the mandible. The oral cavity formed between our upper and lower jaw provides protection for our tongue and upper airway.

Holes in Our Head?

If you examine a skull closely, you will see many, many holes. Some are large, some are small. The most obvious holes in the skull are on the front. These are, of course, our eye sockets. The eye sockets protect our eyes and also provide a passage for the *optic nerves* to connect with the brain. The optic nerves carry the impulses created by what our eyes see to our brain.

You can also see the opening of the nasal passage on the front of the skull as well as the ear canal on either side. This ear canal is also called the *external acoustic meatus* — *external* meaning "outer," *acoustic* meaning "hearing," and *meatus* meaning "opening." You see, even the big words assigned to anatomical structures usually make sense.

At the base of the skull is a very large opening called the *foramen magnum*. *Foramen* means "opening" and *magnum* means "big." Can you guess what this "big opening" is for? Of course you can. Through this opening passes the spinal cord, which is connected to the brainstem. Through the foramen magnum, then, the brain can send signals to and receive information from the body, via the spinal cord.

Beyond these larger openings there are many small holes, each also called a foramen. *Foramina* means more than one foramen. Through these little foramina small *cranial nerves* pass to control your head and neck.

Other important types of "holes" are *sinus cavities*, or *sinuses* for short. These cavities make the skull lighter. Sinuses

Hyoid Bone

Did you know that your tongue has its own bone? The hyoid bone is not in the tongue but under it. Shaped like a horseshoe, this small bone is located in the neck between the jawbone and the thyroid gland. It is the only bone not connected to another bone. Anchored instead by muscles and ligaments to several distant points above, below, and behind, the hyoid bone provides a point of attachment for the muscles of the tongue, the floor of the mouth, the voice box, and many muscles used in swallowing.

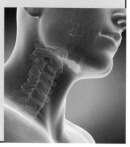

also heat the air we breathe, especially in the winter! Also, if the air you breathe is too dry, the moist linings of the sinuses moisten the air before it reaches the lungs.

The Vertebral Column

The vertebral column is made up of 26 bones and provides a strong central support for our bodies. It not only holds us up, but it is vitally important because it protects the spinal cord as it extends from the base of the brain to the lower back.

This structure must then be very, very strong but also provide enough movement that we can turn our heads, twist to look behind us, bend to pick up our clothes off the floor, and shift to balance as we run up the stairs.

In the vertebral column, our Creator has provided us the means to accomplish all these things!

It is best to think of the vertebral column as being made up of five regions: cervical (neck), thoracic (chest), lumbar (lower back), sacrum, and coccyx. Each part consists of vertebrae, but the intricate shapes of the bones in each section and the way they connect allows each region to function as it should.

The cervical region is composed of 7 vertebral bones (called *vertebrae*). The thoracic region contains 12 vertebrae, and the lumbar region has 5 vertebrae. The sacrum is 1 fused bone that is formed by the fusion of 5 vertebrae. Similarly, the coccyx is 1 fused bone formed from the fusion of 3 to 5 vertebrae.

When you view the spine from the front, it appears relatively straight. However, when viewed from the side, the spine is decidedly curved. In fact, it has several curves, like an S. The curvature of the spine is vitally important to us. If our spine were not curved as it is, we could have difficulty walking with balance or carrying anything heavy. The curve of the spine

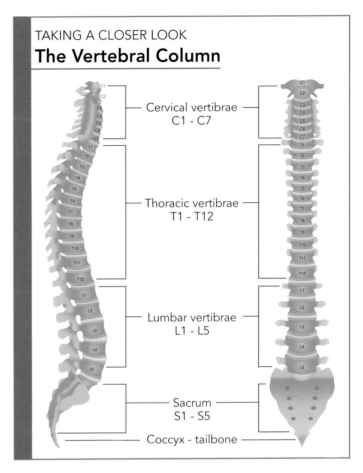

TAKING A CLOSER LOOK
The Vertebral Column

Cervical vertibrae
C1 - C7

Thoracic vertibrae
T1 - T12

Lumbar vertibrae
L1 - L5

Sacrum
S1 - S5

Coccyx - tailbone

actually helps maintain a certain degree of flexibility. This flexibility helps distribute the stresses on the spine as we walk or lift.

Let's take a look at a typical vertebral bone (or *vertebra*).

The front (anterior) part of a vertebra is called the *vertebral body*. This is the largest part of the vertebra.

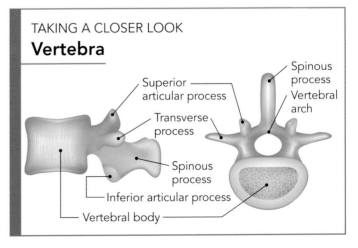

TAKING A CLOSER LOOK
Vertebra

Spinous process
Vertebral arch
Superior articular process
Transverse process
Spinous process
Inferior articular process
Vertebral body

It is basically oval in shape. It is the body of the vertebra that gives the spine its strength. The vertebral body provides support and bears the weight of our body.

To the rear (posterior) of the body of the vertebra is a ring of bone with a foramen (hole) in the center. This is called the vertebral arch. Along the *vertebral arch* extend several projections called *processes*. These bony processes provide attachment points for muscles and ligaments.

The vertebrae are stacked one on top of the other. As you can see from the illustration, vertebrae do increase in size somewhat as you travel down the vertebral column. Cervical vertebrae are smaller than lumbar vertebrae.

The vertebrae are separated by cushions called *intervertebral discs*. These tough, rubbery discs are made of fibrocartilage. The intervertebral discs act as shock absorbers as we walk or run.

In addition, there are very sturdy ligaments along both the front and back of the vertebral column to keep the bones in place and to provide further stability. Without these ligaments the spinal column would be no more stable than a stack of coins. These ligaments keep the stacked vertebrae from sliding off of each other as the spinal column bends and twists.

There is a large hole in each of the vertebrae, called a *vertebral foramen*. The hole is formed by the arch-like projections on the back part of each vertebra. As the vertebrae are stacked one on top of the other, these holes match up to form a long canal, called the vertebral canal. Can you guess what it is for? Of course, this is where the spinal cord is located. This long canal protects the spinal cord as it runs from the base of the brain to the lower back. Between each pair of the vertebrae are small openings called *intervertebral foramina*. (*Inter* means "between." So this word just means "holes between the vertebrae"!)

Is the Back Poorly Designed?

Evolutionists believe that many thousands of years ago, humans walked on all fours. So it is their contention that the human spine is best suited to movement on all fours, and when humans began to walk upright, the spine was no longer ideal. For this reason you will often hear the claim that the back is an example of poor design. Thus, the evolutionist will claim that evolution must be true because there could not be an all-knowing Creator God that would be responsible for such shoddy workmanship.

Actually, nothing could be further from the truth. The human spine is a marvel of design and performs its task very, very well. The curvature of the spine allows the weight of the body to be properly distributed so that we are well-balanced while at the same time providing maximum flexibility to allow us to move efficiently in our environment.

Evolutionists say that humans have lots and lots of back problems because our spine is not designed for walking on two feet. That claim is simply incorrect. The Creator God of the universe knew exactly what He was doing when He designed the human spine.

The problem is that we all live in a fallen, cursed world. Our bodies wear out. Things begin to fail as a result of the decay that occurs in our world. Many factors contribute to the back problems that people suffer from. These factors include such things as improper or excessive lifting, obesity, smoking, and poor posture, to name but a few. Thus, back problems are not a result of poor design, but rather are the result of the effect of sin on our world.

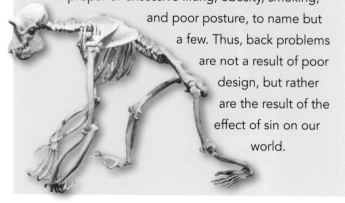

Through these openings, nerves branch out from the spinal cord and go to various parts of the body.

The Thoracic Cage

The axial skeleton not only protects the spinal cord, it also protects the heart and lungs. The heart and lungs are protected inside a thoracic cage. The thoracic cage is made up of the 12 thoracic vertebrae in the rear, the 12 pairs of ribs on the sides, and the *sternum* (breastbone) in the front.

The Ribs

We have 12 pairs of ribs. That's 24 ribs in all. Each rib attaches in the rear to a vertebra. The first seven ribs are called "true" ribs. They are called this because they attach in the front to the sternum. Thus, each pair of true ribs, combined with one thoracic vertebra and a part of the sternum, forms a ring. These ribs are attached to the sternum by flexible connective tissue called *costal cartilage*. This cartilage allows the

ribs to move, rising and falling with every breath. Is this important? It's actually very important if you want to breathe. You see, the rib cage expands and contracts during respiration. As we breathe in, our rib cage expands. As we exhale our rib cage contracts.

Ribs eight through ten are called "false ribs." This is kind of an unfortunate description because they really are ribs. They are called "false ribs" because they do not directly attach to the sternum in the front. Rather, in the front, these ribs attach to the costal cartilage above them. Thus, they do have an attachment and form part of the continuous expanding and contracting wall of the thoracic cage, but the attachment to the sternum is more indirect.

Ribs 11 and 12 are called "floating ribs." They don't really float, because they are attached to thoracic vertebrae in the back. The term "floating" refers to the fact they have no attachment in the front.

The Sternum

The front portion of the thoracic cage is the sternum, or breastbone. As was noted previously, rib pairs one through seven attach to the sternum by means of costal cartilages. This bone is quite strong and helps provide protection to the heart and lungs.

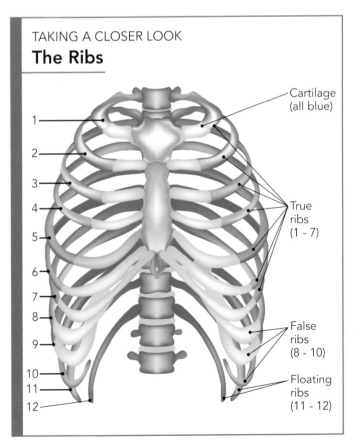

TAKING A CLOSER LOOK
The Ribs

1
2
3
4
5
6
7
8
9
10
11
12

Cartilage (all blue)

True ribs (1 - 7)

False ribs (8 - 10)

Floating ribs (11 - 12)

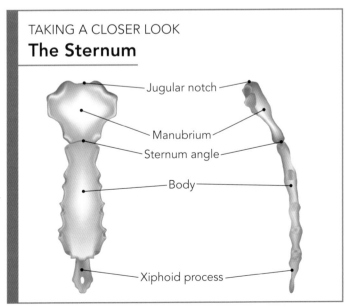

TAKING A CLOSER LOOK
The Sternum

Jugular notch

Manubrium

Sternum angle

Body

Xiphoid process

The Appendicular Skeleton

The appendicular skeleton is made up of the upper and lower limbs and the "girdles" that attach them to the body. The appendicular skeleton allows us to both move around in our environment (via our lower extremities) and interact with our environment (via our upper extremities). Of the total of 206 bones in our body, 126 bones are found in the appendicular skeleton.

Do Men Have Fewer Ribs Than Women?

Over the years, many people have been taught that women have one more rib than men. This is due to what the Bible tells us about the creation of Eve.

"And the LORD God caused a deep sleep to fall on Adam, and he slept; and He took one of his ribs, and closed up the flesh in its place. Then the rib which the LORD God had taken from man He made into a woman, and He brought her to the man" (Genesis 2:21–22).

So if the Lord took a rib from Adam to make Eve, then women should have more ribs than men, right? Actually, no. Both men and women have 12 pairs of ribs. It is very easy to demonstrate. All you need to do is count the number of ribs in a man and in a woman, and there you have it.

It simply comes down to this. Removing a rib from Adam did not mean that his children would have one less rib. After all, in Adam's DNA is the information to code for 12 pairs of ribs, so the children should have 12 pairs of ribs.

So, as is usually the case, it's all in our DNA.

The Upper Limb

The upper limb consists of the pectoral (or shoulder) girdle, arm, forearm, wrist, and hand.

The Pectoral Girdle

The pair of bones that attaches each upper limb to the body is called a pectoral girdle. Some people call it the "shoulder girdle." Both terms are correct.

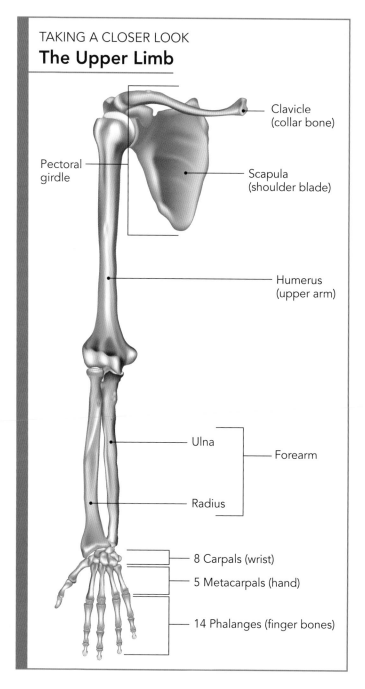

TAKING A CLOSER LOOK
The Upper Limb

- Clavicle (collar bone)
- Pectoral girdle
- Scapula (shoulder blade)
- Humerus (upper arm)
- Ulna
- Radius
- Forearm
- 8 Carpals (wrist)
- 5 Metacarpals (hand)
- 14 Phalanges (finger bones)

The pectoral girdle consists of the *clavicle* (collarbone) and the *scapula* (shoulder blade). The clavicle attaches at one end to the sternum and to the scapula at the other end. Interestingly enough, the scapula does not directly attach to anything but the clavicle. The scapula does not attach to the axial skeleton. Instead, the scapula is attached to the body by a series of muscles. This is a good thing in many ways. The main advantage of this design is that it allows the scapula to move more freely. This allows much more movement of our arms.

However, the more movement or flexibility a joint has, the less stable it is. So there is a price to pay for the amazing range of motion. The shoulder joint is not as stable as many other joints in the body.

The Arm

You are probably accustomed to thinking of your upper limb as your "arm," but in actual anatomical terms, your *arm* is only the part between your shoulder and elbow. The part between elbow and wrist is the *forearm*. Therefore, there is only *one* bone in your arm: the *humerus*. The humerus forms a ball-and-socket joint with the shoulder on the top and a hinge joint with the forearm's *ulna* below, at the elbow.

The Forearm

The forearm consists of two bones: the *radius* and the *ulna*. The radius is the one on the same side as your thumb. The bones attach on one end to the humerus to form the elbow and on the other end to the wrist.

SO SIMPLE YET Designed by the Master SO COMPLEX

The Dislocated Shoulder

The shoulder joint has the greatest range of movement of any joint in the body. Its amazing design gives us the ability to move our arms in almost any direction. However, the trade-off for all this flexibility is that the shoulder joint is much more unstable than other joints. This makes the shoulder susceptible to injury, especially dislocation.

A shoulder dislocation is a situation where the ball-shaped upper end of the humerus is separated from the shallow, bowl-shaped depression in the scapula (called the *glenoid fossa*). (This ball-and-socket joint is called the *glenohumeral joint*.) The most common form of shoulder dislocation is where the humerus is displaced forward, or *anteriorly*, called an anterior dislocation. This is usually the result of a fall where a person lands on an outstretched arm, pushing the top of the arm bone forward and out of its socket.

When a dislocation occurs, the goal of treatment is obviously to return the shoulder to its normal position. There are a variety of techniques that can be used to coax the shoulder back into position. If this is successful, then the arm is usually placed in a sling for a period of time. Then strengthening exercises and physical therapy can help the shoulder recover its strength.

In the most severe cases, shoulder dislocations can require surgery to correct. In these more extreme cases, the recovery time is certainly much longer.

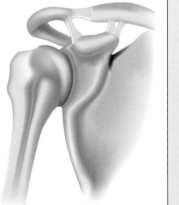
Normal shoulder anatomy

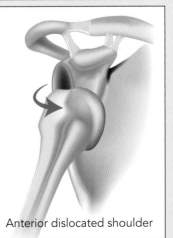
Anterior dislocated shoulder

At the elbow, the *proximal* end of the ulna and the *distal* end of the humerus form a hinge joint. This part of the elbow is primarily concerned with flexion/extension movement. At the elbow, the proximal end of the radius forms a pivot joint rather than a hinge joint. This joint allows the rotation of the forearm.

Try this. Put your finger on the tip of your elbow. This is the proximal end of the ulna and is called the *olecranon*. Now rotate your forearm. You will notice the olecranon does not move. This is because this rotation movement involves the radius and not the ulna. (When you whack the nerve that runs close to this bone, it hurts in a particular way that most of us don't like, and we say we hit our "funny bone.")

The Wrist and Hand

The human hand is an engineering marvel. Its movements are so varied that we can grip a bat, put spin on a ball, or play the violin. Our hands are strong enough that we can grip a hammer to drive a nail, yet they are so delicate that we can hold a baby bird

without crushing it or pick up a tiny pin. Only a wise Designer could create something like our hands!

But here is something to think about. On each side, in the wrist and hand, are 27 bones. Just think of that! In combination, the wrists and hands have a total of 54 bones out of the 206 bones in our bodies! Considering that, they must be pretty important, right? You bet they are! How could we do all the incredible things humans do without our hands!

In the wrist are 8 bones called *carpal bones*. These are stacked in two rows containing four bones each. Just move your wrist around to see how this arrangement allows so much movement!

Next we have five bones called *metacarpals*, one for each digit in our hand (clever, huh?). These are the bones in the palm of our hand. These allow some movement, but not nearly as much as our fingers. Finally, we have the bones of the thumb and fingers. These are called phalanges; each finger has three phalanges, the thumb has only two.

Wow, what an intricate collection of bones and joints! Just think of how incredible your arms (oops, I mean, your upper limbs) are.

The Lower Limb

The lower limb consists of the pelvic girdle (or just the "pelvis"), thigh, leg, ankle, and foot. You probably thought the leg started at your hip, but in anatomic terms it doesn't. The *thigh* — with only one bone — connects the hip and the knee. The *leg* — with two bones — begins at the knee and goes to the ankle.

The Pelvic Girdle

The pelvic girdle is the structure that attaches the lower limbs to the body. The pelvis consists of two hipbones and the sacrum, which is part of the vertebral column. The hipbones have a large

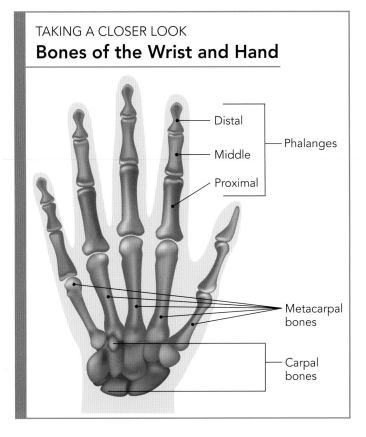

TAKING A CLOSER LOOK
Bones of the Wrist and Hand

Distal
Middle — Phalanges
Proximal

Metacarpal bones

Carpal bones

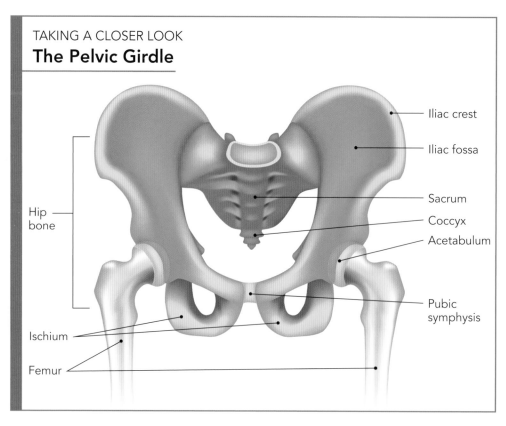

Iliac crest

Iliac fossa

Sacrum

Coccyx

Acetabulum

Pubic symphysis

Hip bone

Ischium

Femur

There is only one bone in the thigh, and it is called the *femur*. The femur is the longest and strongest bone in the body. It has to be to endure the stress that is placed on it. This bone has to withstand the stress that comes with all the running and jumping and lifting that we all do each day.

The femur attaches to the pelvis at the hip joint. The ball of the femur fits into a special cavity on the pelvis known as the *acetabulum*. A complex set of ligaments holds this joint in place. Can you guess what type of joint this is? Sure you can, it is a ball-and-socket joint!

wing-like prominence on each side, called the iliac crest. You can feel this just below your waist on each side. The hipbones are connected to the sacrum in the back. They are connected to each other in front with a fibrocartilage joint called the *pubic symphysis*. (Remember, this is a cartilaginous joint as we described earlier.) Below the sacrum is the tip of the vertebral column, the *coccyx* (sometimes called the tailbone).

This structure is thus attached to the axial skeleton, and it connects the lower limbs by means of the hip joint. The pelvis is like a large, strong bowl, open in the bottom. It is a sturdy ring that bears the weight of the upper body. It also protects the organs that are located in the pelvis. And the strong muscles lining the pelvis close the bottom of the bowl to keep your insides from falling through.

The Thigh

The thigh is the section of the lower limb from the hip to the knee.

The lower end of the femur makes up part of the knee joint.

The Leg

The leg is the part of the lower limb from the knee to the ankle. The leg is composed of two bones, the tibia and the fibula. These two bones help form the knee joint at one end and the ankle at the other. The tibia, or shinbone, is the larger of the two bones and bears almost all of the weight. The fibula does not bear any significant amount of the body's weight. That does not mean it is unimportant. The fibula provides a place of attachment for several muscles, and it forms the outer part of the ankle joint.

The Ankle and Foot

Just as with the wrist and hand, the ankle and foot are composed of many bones. On each side in the ankle and foot are 26 bones. So our ankles and feet altogether have 52 bones! Again, this indicates the complex nature of our feet and ankles. Without them we could not walk or move as effortlessly as we do. Just like our hands, our ankles and feet are engineering marvels.

The ankle is made up of the distal ends of the tibia and fibula, along with one of the tarsal bones in the foot, called the *talus*. You can feel a rounded part of the fibula on the outside of your ankle and a rounded part of the tibia on the inside of your ankle. Although not quite as flexible as the wrist, the ankle is quite mobile in its own right.

The posterior portion of the foot is composed of seven bones called tarsals.

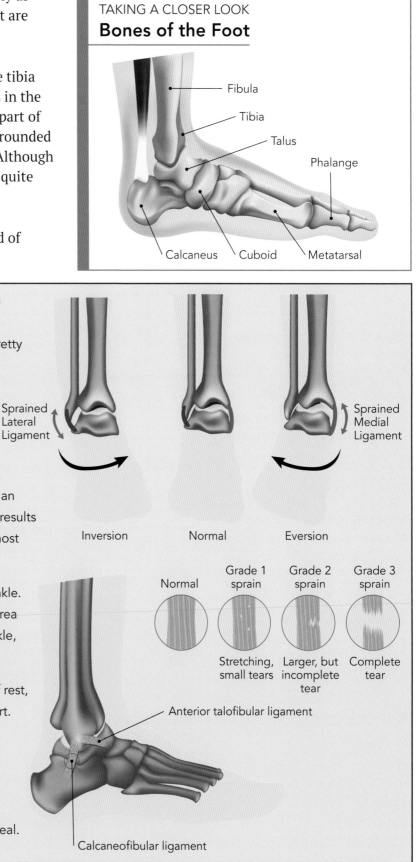

TAKING A CLOSER LOOK
Bones of the Foot

Fibula
Tibia
Talus
Phalange
Calcaneus   Cuboid   Metatarsal

What Is a Sprained Ankle?

Lots of folks have sprained their ankles. It's a pretty common injury.

So what is a sprain exactly?

An ankle sprain is a situation where a ligament in the ankle is torn. A severe twisting or turning of the ankle causes a sprain. Perhaps the most common cause of a sprain is an inward twisting (or inversion) of the ankle. This results in a tear in one of the ligaments in the ankle (most often the *anterior talofibular ligament*).

This injury results in pain and swelling of the ankle. There is often bruising or discoloration in the area of the injury. If you have ever sprained your ankle, you know how uncomfortable it can be.

Treatment of an ankle sprain usually consists of rest, intermittent ice packs, and some sort of support. The support can be a walking boot, an elastic wrap, or even a small air cast.

Most ankle sprains heal in two to four weeks. However, depending on the severity of the sprain, some injuries can take up to a year to heal.

Sprained Lateral Ligament

Sprained Medial Ligament

Inversion   Normal   Eversion

Normal   Grade 1 sprain   Grade 2 sprain   Grade 3 sprain

Stretching, small tears   Larger, but incomplete tear   Complete tear

Anterior talofibular ligament

Calcaneofibular ligament

One of these bones helps form the ankle joint as just mentioned. Another of the tarsal bones is called the *calcaneus*, the heel bone.

The mid-portion of the foot (again like the hand) is composed of five bones; these are called *metatarsals*. And again, as in the hand, the toes are made of three phalanges each, save for the big toe, which has only two.

The tarsals and metatarsals are each shaped and arranged to work together. They are strapped together by many ligaments, tendons, and sheets of tough connective tissue, but they are strapped together just loosely enough to allow them to shift a little. Does this seem strange? Well, if the bones in the foot didn't give a little, you would have a hard time walking and running smoothly.

When you take a step, you plant your heel and rock forward. As the heel strikes the ground, the joints between the bones in the foot loosen just a little. They loosen *just enough* to allow the foot to change its overall shape as the weight above it shifts during the beginning of each step. Then the bones shift again, sliding into place against each other and interlocking to form a somewhat rigid lever. That lever helps you transfer your body's weight forward during the last part of your step.

These slight movements between the foot's bones also allow the foot to constantly change shape enough to remain stable as we walk or run across uneven surfaces. Tough ligaments in the foot help our feet bear all the weight from the thousands of steps we take each day, keeping its many bones in their proper positions as they do all that shifting and interlocking.

An important feature of the human foot is the arch. Actually, the foot has several arches. But most people think of its easy-to-see longitudinal arch from front to back. The ligaments and other connective tissue maintain the foot's arches. Take a look at your foot

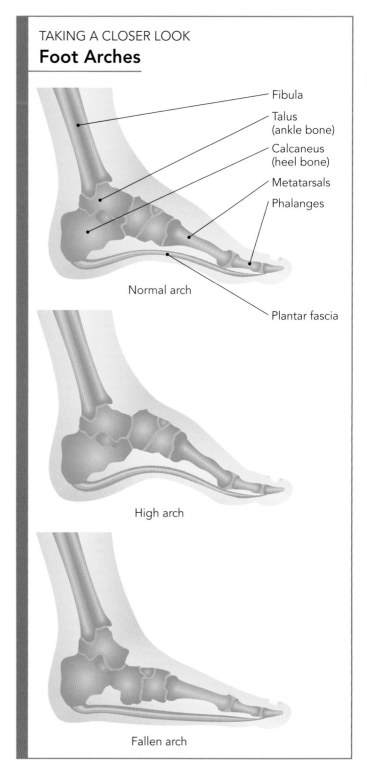

TAKING A CLOSER LOOK
Foot Arches

Fibula

Talus (ankle bone)

Calcaneus (heel bone)

Metatarsals

Phalanges

Normal arch

Plantar fascia

High arch

Fallen arch

starting at the base of the big toe and moving toward your heel. See the curve in your foot? That is the longitudinal arch. This curve keeps part of the foot up off the ground. This is a better arrangement for people than a flatter foot would be because we walk upright on two legs. God designed us to walk that

Bipedal People

God designed human beings to walk upright on two legs. This is called a bipedal gait. The most efficient way for humans to walk is upright. Apes are designed to move through trees using their hands and feet, to climb while gripping branches with their feet, to walk along branches, and also to move along the ground. An ape can walk on two legs for a time, but a two-legged walk is not an efficient way for an ape to walk.

Some people claim that humans evolved from ape-like ancestors. They say they learned to walk upright and, having hands free to use tools and explore the world, eventually developed larger, smarter brains and became human. Of course, walking on two legs could never make it possible for an ape-like animal to become a more human-like one. There have never been any ape-men, only apes and humans. God made the first man and woman in His own image on the same day He made apes and monkeys. He did not use evolution.

When evolutionists find fossilized bones belonging to extinct apes (like the australopithecine ape they call "Lucy"), they often claim that the bones show the extinct apes were bipedal evolutionary ancestors of humans. But fossils do not walk. Even when paleontologists find lots of bones, despite the claims of evolutionists, those shapes do not show that the ape was truly bipedal. Sometimes paleontologists also find fossilized footprints. You may have heard of the fossilized Laetoli footprints found in Africa. Evolutionists claim the footprints were made by a family of our ape-like ancestors. But we know that the footprints were made by human beings, because they show the feet had arches! Only human feet have arches, because only human feet were designed for a lifetime of walking upright on two feet!

way, with the muscles and bones in our hips, legs, and feet all working together.

The foot's arches are important because when you walk, you push your weight off of your toes and you land with your weight on your heel. This is repeated with each step. The longitudinal arch provides both support and flexibility to your feet. When you step, the arch stretches a little, making walking much more efficient. In a way, you might say the arches in your feet give you a "spring" in your step!

Walking from Head to Toe

Many features of the human skeleton make walking upright on two legs just right for humans. The way the skull attaches to the neck makes looking forward comfortable for us. The way the muscles and bones of the hip are arranged allows us to step forward without swinging our thighs out to the side. The curves in the back, which develop once a child begins walking but are made possible by the shapes of the vertebrae, help us keep our balance. The way our arms attach to our shoulders allows them to swing just right, helping us shift our weight smoothly from one leg to the other. The way the bones in the foot constantly shift just enough to allow the foot to change shape as we begin each step helps us adjust to bear our constantly shifting body weight. The way those same bones then slide into a locking position transforms the foot into a rigid lever to propel our upright body forward.

It is amazing how the bones, ligaments, and muscles in the hips, legs, and feet are all arranged at just the right angle to make the bones in the foot slide into the optimal positions to become semi-rigid during the last part of every step. The arches of the foot make it springy enough to bear our weight through hours of standing and walking but allow the foot to become that rigid lever needed to walk upright efficiently. If the foot had no arch, it would bend like an ape's foot with every step, making it difficult to propel the body forward.

THE MUSCULAR SYSTEM

Now that we've seen what a busy place a bone is, you'll never again think a skeleton is just a frame to give your body shape. A lot is going on inside your bones. But as cool as our skeletons are, they really aren't going anywhere on their own. They are going to need some serious help. We need to learn about muscles. Without muscles, all this stuff about bones and joints would not mean a thing. Muscles cover your skeleton and help give you the movement you need!

Muscle cars. Muscle builders. Strength is often associated with muscles. The stronger our muscles the more we can often endure, the more we can lift, and the more weight we can move. So let's see what the muscle is made of, the characteristics of muscle, the different types of muscle, what it is they do to move you, and more! With over 600 muscles in the body, you're bound to discover a few amazing things about how God designed you and formed you for His beautiful purpose for your life.

"Have I not commanded you? Be strong and of good courage; do not be afraid, nor be dismayed, for the Lord your God is with you wherever you go" (Joshua 1:9).

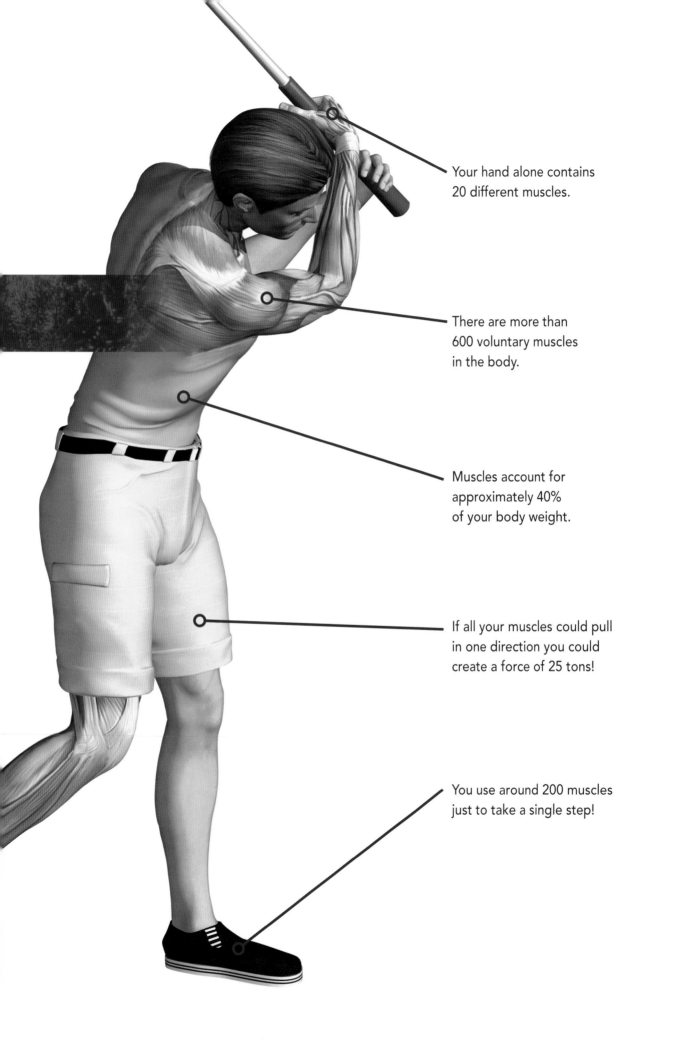

Your hand alone contains 20 different muscles.

There are more than 600 voluntary muscles in the body.

Muscles account for approximately 40% of your body weight.

If all your muscles could pull in one direction you could create a force of 25 tons!

You use around 200 muscles just to take a single step!

MUSCLE BASICS

Muscles do one thing: they contract. *Contract* means get smaller or shorter. Muscles pull on whatever is attached to them when they contract. And even though *you* are able to pull and push on things, *your muscles can only pull. A muscle cannot push.* Does that surprise you? We'll see later that many muscles are paired to pull in opposite directions, but each muscle itself can only pull. By contracting, muscles perform an amazing variety of jobs.

Skull

Hand

Knee

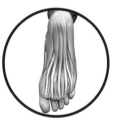
Foot

Because some muscles are attached on each end to bones, their contraction makes those bones move. The kind of movement that happens depends on where the muscles are attached. Throwing, running, swimming, playing the piano — all are movements produced when particular combinations of muscles contract. Without muscles, we wouldn't be going anywhere.

When the muscle tissue that makes up your heart contracts, your heart squeezes and pumps blood. Muscles in the wall of your digestive tract propel your food along its way as it is digested. Muscle tissue in the ureters help push urine into the bladder.

Second, muscles help to maintain your upright posture. Without the continuing activity of muscles along your spine, in your abdomen, in the neck, and attached to your pelvis, you could not stay upright against the constant pull of gravity. You would just fall down in a heap!

Next, muscle help strengthen our joints. The tension generated by muscles helps keep our joints strong and stable.

Muscle contraction also generates heat. One of the ways we can stay warm in cold weather is from the heat generated by our muscles. If you have ever stood outside on a very cold day, you might have begun to shiver. This shivering is due to muscle contractions. This is a way the body generates heat to keep you warm.

Characteristics of Muscle

The most obvious characteristic of muscle tissue is its *contractility*. This means it can contract, or shorten, with great force. No other tissue does this.

The next characteristic is its *elasticity*. This means that when a muscle is stretched, it has the ability to return to its resting length. In other words, it can recoil.

Another characteristic is *excitability*. This means that muscle can respond to a stimulus or a trigger. For example, a muscle cell can be stimulated to contract by a signal from a nerve cell, or from a chemical messenger.

The last characteristic is *extensibility*. This means that muscle can be stretched. When relaxed, muscle can even be stretched beyond its resting length when circumstances dictate.

Muscle is quite amazing, isn't it!

SO SIMPLE YET Designed by the Master SO COMPLEX

Movement

Have you ever stopped to consider just how lucky we are? Our bodies have been designed to allow us to move around in our environment. How dull would it be if we were like trees or flowers and had to stay in the same place our whole life?

Our wonderful Creator has given us the privilege of moving freely in the world He made for us. We can walk, run, climb, or swim.

Not only have we been designed to move about in the world, we have the ability to interact with the world and the people around us. We can hold a pen to write a letter. We can move our lips to speak. We can use a hammer to build a new doghouse for our favorite pet. It goes on and on.

Our muscles make all these things possible. It is just one more reason that we should always stop and give praise to our Creator, the One who made our incredible bodies!

Types of Muscle

In our discussion of tissue types, we saw that there are three types of muscle: skeletal muscle, cardiac muscle, and smooth muscle. Let's review these again.

Skeletal muscle is the kind of muscle that moves the body. These muscles attach to the skeleton, and their contraction causes the bones to move and propel the body. Skeletal muscles also make good posture possible. This type of muscle accounts for about 40 percent of our body mass.

Skeletal muscle is also known as *voluntary muscle*. This means that skeletal muscle contracts on your command. You can consciously control it. If you want to open a door, your brain sends a signal down nerve fibers to the muscles telling your upper limb to reach forward. Then your brain sends nerve signals to the muscles in your hand to grab the doorknob and twist it.

Also, skeletal muscle is *striated*, which means "striped." A distinctive pattern of stripes is visible under the microscope. We will see why later.

Smooth muscle is found in the walls of most hollow organs in the body. It is in the walls of the stomach, the urinary bladder, the blood vessels, and even respiratory passages. Smooth muscle is involuntary, so it contracts without your having to consciously think about it. We will not deal with smooth muscle here but will discuss smooth muscle in more detail when we explore other organ systems.

Cardiac muscle is the third type of muscle. As we have mentioned, this type of muscle is found only in the heart. It is also involuntary muscle, although cardiac muscle is striated and has some similarities to skeletal muscle. However, there are also distinct differences. We will examine these differences when we study the cardiovascular system.

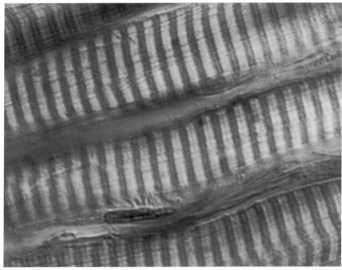

Photomicrograph of skeletal muscle

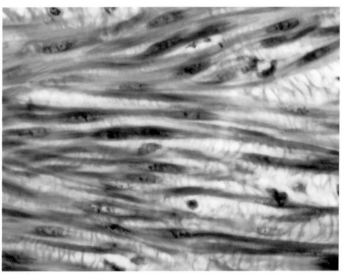

Photomicrograph of smooth muscle

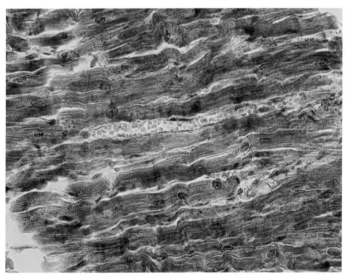

Photomicrograph of cardiac muscle

Skeletal Muscle Structure

To better understand how skeletal muscles work, we need to see how muscle tissue is organized. Let's start with a cross section of a typical skeletal muscle so that we can see how muscle cells are bundled together and how those bundles are bundled together. Because muscle tissue is organized in bundles and bundles of bundles, its parts can work together very efficiently.

A muscle cell is long and thin, like a string, so another name for a muscle cell is a *muscle fiber*. A bundle of muscle fibers wrapped in a connective tissue sheath is called a fascicle. The fibers in a fascicle all contract at the same time. The muscle is composed of many fascicles.

Remember, a *muscle fiber* is the same thing as a *muscle cell*. A muscle fiber can be very long, often extending the entire length of the muscle. The longest muscle fibers are in the thigh muscles. We think of cells as very small things, but the muscle cells, or muscle fibers, in the thigh can be 12 inches long. Each muscle cell is surrounded by its own connective tissue sheath, and then each fascicle is bundled together by another connective tissue sheath.

All the connective tissue sheaths in a muscle are continuous with one another. In addition, they extend on each end of the muscle to the *tendons* that attach the muscle to the bones. (Remember, ligaments attach bones to bones, and tendons attach muscles to bones.) When the muscle fibers contract, this force is ultimately transmitted through the network of connected connective tissue sheaths to the tendons, and the bones are thus moved.

Muscles need a lot of fuel and oxygen to do their work. Therefore, muscles must have a very rich blood supply. Blood brings oxygen and sugar and other important materials to the muscle and removes the waste products generated by all the muscle activity. Without a good blood supply, muscle fibers wouldn't have the fuel and oxygen to efficiently produce the energy to move.

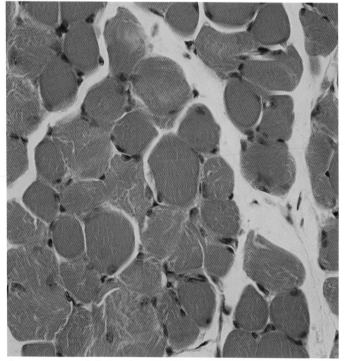

Cross section of skeletal muscle

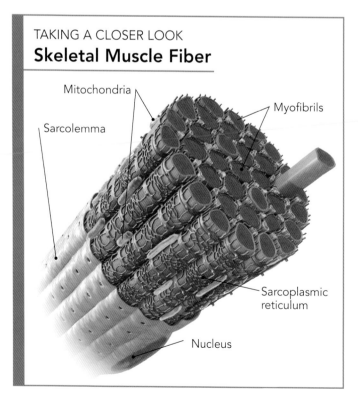

TAKING A CLOSER LOOK
Skeletal Muscle Fiber

Mitochondria

Myofibrils

Sarcolemma

Sarcoplasmic reticulum

Nucleus

Organized to Move

As we noted, a skeletal muscle fiber is the same thing as a skeletal muscle cell. Each long cell has more than one nucleus and many mitochondria. Each also contains many special protein molecules called *actin* and *myosin*. Muscles cells are only able to contact because of the way actin and myosin molecules tug on each other. Let's zoom out to see how each muscle cell is organized to take advantage of the unusual properties of actin and myosin molecules.

Many of the words describing muscles and their parts contain the prefix "myo." Remember that we said words that begin with the prefix "osteo" refer to bone. Well, words that begin with the prefix "myo" refer to muscle. Thus you see that one of the important molecules that makes a muscle contract — *myosin* — begins with "myo."

Myofilament is another of those important "myo" words. *Myofilaments* can be made of myosin molecules or actin molecules, and there are a lot of myofilaments in every muscle fiber. *Thick myofilaments* are made of myosin. *Thin myofilaments* are made of actin. They are arranged like cordwood next to each other. When a muscle fiber is stimulated to contract, the thick and thin myofilaments slide past each other because of the way actin and myosin molecules interact.

Of course, just a few bundles of molecules tugging past each other wouldn't move your leg. It takes a lot of

them and they must be organized just so in order to work together. The simplest *contractile unit* of a muscle is called the *sarcomere*. That means that each sarcomere contracts. Each sarcomere is made of thick and thin myofilaments. Sarcomeres attached end-to-end are called *myofibrils*. There's another "myo" word! Because each sarcomere contracts, and the sarcomeres are attached end-to-end, the myofibril contracts. Hundreds of myofibrils are packed into each muscle fiber, or cell. And of course each muscle contains many such cells.

Thus, we see that each muscle fiber is made of myofibrils. Myofibrils are made of sarcomeres hooked end to end. And each myofibril is made of thick and thin myofilaments. Those myofilaments are made of

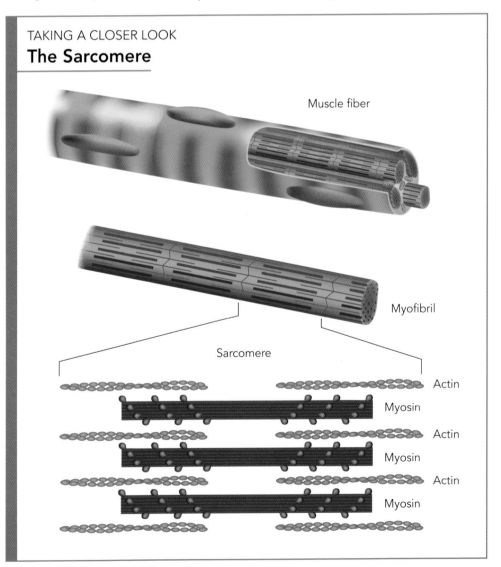

TAKING A CLOSER LOOK
The Sarcomere

Muscle fiber

Myofibril

Sarcomere

Actin
Myosin
Actin
Myosin
Actin
Myosin

actin and myosin. (We'll learn more about how those molecules work soon.) In the illustration, you can see how these parts are arranged.

Remember we said that muscle is striped, or *striated*? Skeletal muscle looks striped under the microscope because of the alternating pattern of thin/thick/thin filaments.

Stimulated to Move

This organization of the myofibrils is vitally important to the function of muscle tissue. It is the interaction of the actin and myosin that produces the contraction of muscle. You see in the illustration that the thick myofilament, made of myosin, has small "heads" along its length. These heads can actually form links with the thin actin myofibrils and pull them in a fashion that shortens the sarcomere. When each sarcomere in a fiber contracts, the muscle fiber itself obviously

contracts! And because each fiber and each bundle of fibers is wrapped in connective tissue that extends into the tendon attaching the muscle to the structure (like a bone) it is supposed to move, the contraction of those strings of sarcomeres is translated into a movement of the entire muscle. Simply, this is how a muscle works.

Well, as it turns out, it's not really that simple.

You remember that skeletal muscle is voluntary muscle. That is, it moves when you want it to.

So, let's back up to the beginning. You know, to the "I want to move my hand!" part, and take it step by step.

First of all, you decide, "I want to move my hand!" The part of your brain that controls muscle activity sends a signal, through the spinal cord, to the nerves going to the hand. (We will examine how this nerve impulse travels when we study the nervous system. For now, think of the message getting sent along a nerve like a line of dominoes falling down.)

When the nerve signal reaches a muscle fiber (a muscle cell), another signal is generated in the muscle fiber itself. This signal causes calcium to pour out of an organelle called the *sarcoplasmic reticulum*. Remember when we studied the parts of a cell? You may recall a structure called *smooth endoplasmic reticulum*. The sarcoplasmic reticulum is merely the specialized form of smooth endoplasmic reticulum found in muscle cells. It is designed to store large amounts of calcium.

TAKING A CLOSER LOOK
Actin and Myosin Interaction

Myosin head — P — ADP — Thin filamanet (actin)
Thick filamanet (myosin)
Cross-bridge
ATP

You see, in this sequence, calcium is the key. When calcium is released into the muscle fiber, it binds to specific sites on its actin myofilaments. The binding of calcium triggers the myofilament surface to change shape. When the thin myofilaments change shape, myosin molecules in the thick myofilaments can connect to the actin myofilament, forming what is called a *cross bridge*. When this attachment is made, the heads of the myosin then flex and pull the actin, causing contraction. This is called the *sliding filament model* of muscle contraction. (Well, I guess that wasn't so terribly complicated, was it?)

When a muscle fiber is stimulated to contract, the entire fiber contracts. That is, all the sarcomeres in a muscle fiber contract or none of them do. This is called the *all-or-none law*. There is no way for a single muscle fiber to be partially contracted.

One more thing — this entire process takes energy. Lots of energy. That is why muscle cells have so many mitochondria. Mitochondria are the power-houses of cells. They convert fuel, like sugars, into usable energy, constantly recharging each cell's "batteries" so the fiber has the energy to contract. Lots of mitochondria are packed into each fiber to provide plenty of energy for active muscle.

As long as nerve stimulation is applied, calcium is released into the muscle fiber causing contraction. But muscles need to relax also, don't they? Obviously, they do. So how does this happen? Relaxation of the muscle occurs when the nerve stimulation to the muscle stops.

When a muscle fiber is no longer receiving nerve signals, there is no further stimulation of the sarcoplasmic reticulum to release calcium. In fact, without nerve stimulation, the sarcoplasmic reticulum actually pumps the calcium back inside itself. Then calcium is not available to trigger muscle contraction. So the muscle fibers in the muscle relax, and the muscle relaxes.

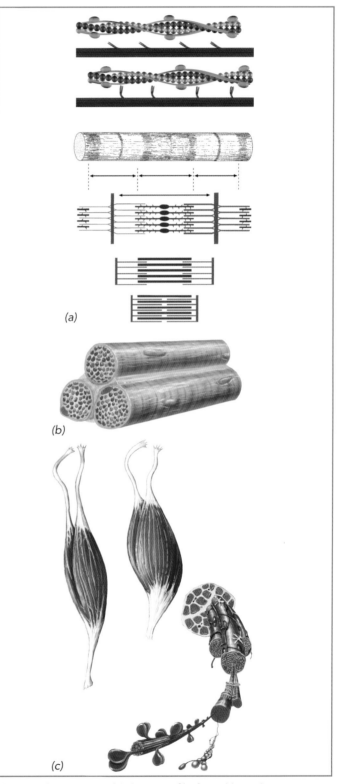

(a)

(b)

(c)

The muscle structure showing myofibrils and how they are bound together to form muscle fibers, then muscles. (a) Muscle cells contain many myofibrils, organelles that are composed of actin and myosin bound together end to end. (b) The myofibrils are secured at either end to the cell membrane. A group of cells are then bound together to form a muscle fiber. (c) Many fibers are in turn bound to form muscle tissue.

Energy to Move

To move our body around, we need lots of energy. Just carrying the weight of your body around from day to day takes an enormous amount of energy. Even holding your body upright in a sitting or standing position instead of flopping over like a rag doll takes energy. How much more energy is needed to play sports or clean your room or ride your bike! We need to take a closer look at how muscles get the energy they require.

The first process by which muscles generate energy is called *aerobic respiration*. Aerobic respiration takes place through a series of chemical reactions that *require oxygen*. That is why it is called *aerobic*. (Do you see that "aer" is sort of like the word *air*, which is where we get our oxygen?) In aerobic respiration the energy stored in a sugar, called *glucose*, is used to generate a special energy storage molecule called adenosine triphosphate (ATP). This process of producing ATP takes place in the mitochondria of the cell. Since muscle cells require so much energy, is it any wonder that they each contain many mitochondria?

Glucose (in the presence of oxygen) is broken down into water and carbon dioxide. This process generates energy. When you build a campfire, you burn wood as a fuel, in the presence of oxygen, to get heat energy. But inside each cell, the energy produced from the fuel (glucose) must be captured and stored so it can be used. The energy produced by "burning" glucose would be useless without a way to store it. That is where ATP comes into the picture.

In aerobic respiration, the energy released from the breakdown of glucose is used to turn a molecule called adenosine diphosphate (ADP) into ATP. This is done by attaching an additional phosphate group (P) to ADP. Adding a phosphate group (P) converts adenosine diphosphate (ADP) to adenosine *triphosphate* (ATP). The key here is the additional phosphate. The chemical bone that attaches the phosphate contains a lot of stored energy.

Now when a muscle cell needs energy, it breaks down ATP into ADP. With the release of the phosphate group (P), energy stored in that chemical bond is released for the cell to use.

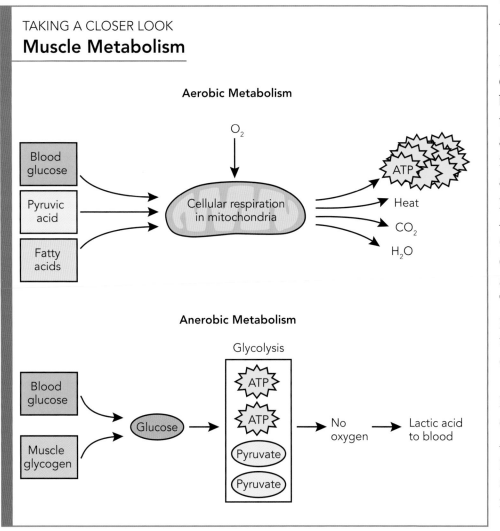

TAKING A CLOSER LOOK
Muscle Metabolism

Aerobic Metabolism

O_2

Blood glucose

Pyruvic acid

Fatty acids

Cellular respiration in mitochondria

ATP

Heat

CO_2

H_2O

Anerobic Metabolism

Glycolysis

Blood glucose

Muscle glycogen

Glucose

ATP

ATP

Pyruvate

Pyruvate

No oxygen

Lactic acid to blood

One way to understand this is to think of ATP as a charged battery in the cell. When the cell uses its stored energy, ATP becomes ADP, which is like an uncharged battery. When this uncharged battery (ADP) is recharged, it becomes ATP.

The problem is that this process of aerobic respiration does not happen instantly. It takes a little time. It does generate lots of ATP, but it takes time. So what if you need lots of ATP quickly? You then need *anaerobic respiration*.

Anaerobic respiration is the process where glucose is broken down *without oxygen being present*. This can take place very quickly, but it does not produce as much ATP as aerobic respiration does. Anaerobic provides a quick burst of energy to get movement started, providing the time needed to generate the large amounts of ATP needed for sustained activity.

In the process of breaking down glucose to generate ATP, anaerobic respiration does not produce water and carbon dioxide like aerobic respiration does. Instead, it produces something called *lactic acid*. Lactic acid diffuses out of the muscle cells and into the blood to be disposed of. However, if anaerobic respiration goes on too long, then a great deal of lactic acid is generated. In that case, the lactic acid can build up in the muscle cells, causing the muscle to become fatigued.

When you exercise regularly, your muscles can actually develop an improved network of capillaries to deliver oxygen-rich blood more efficiently. Then the oxygen you need for quick and prolonged muscle activity can reach the muscle fibers quickly and in large quantities. That way the muscle fibers can use aerobic respiration to generate a lot more energy from glucose. These capillaries also carry away the lactic acid quickly, preventing fatigue. Thus, when you are "in shape," your muscles produce more energy and don't tire as quickly.

What Is a Muscle Cramp?

Have you ever gotten a muscle cramp while you were exercising? It really hurts, doesn't it? Exercise-related muscle cramps can happen when muscle fatigue causes the nervous system to *overstimulate* the muscle. Muscles are more likely to become fatigued if you exercise when you are dehydrated or your body is salt-depleted. Muscle fatigue can also result from a temporary build-up of *lactic acid* in muscles during fast sprinting or heavy exercise that requires the muscles to rely on *anaerobic metabolism*. Lack of regular exercise can also cause muscles to fatigue more easily and cramp. The best thing to do if you get a cramp is to *very gently* stretch the muscles. About half a minute of gentle stretching can reduce the excessive stimulation of the muscle and stop the cramp. Be gentle and don't stretch a cramping muscle too far or forcefully, however, or you may damage the muscle.

Muscle Growth and Performance

Your body is designed to work and exercise. In fact, exercising and using your muscles is the best thing you can do to stay healthy. Lots of activity helps bones and muscles stay strong. It makes your heart and lungs work more efficiently. Most people even say that they think more clearly when they exercise regularly! Now I won't say that regular exercise will make you a straight A student, but it couldn't hurt, right?

Since in this section we are mainly concerned with muscle tissue, what happens to muscle when you exercise? How does muscle grow?

Well, when you exercise regularly, you put your muscles under stress. The muscles respond to this stress by becoming bigger and stronger or by increasing in endurance. How this occurs is interesting.

If you want to increase your endurance, you might begin running, biking, or swimming. Here, muscle is put under less stress, but for longer periods of time. For the most part, these types of exercises do not cause muscle to increase in size. They help increase muscle endurance by increasing the number of mitochondria in the muscle tissue. In addition, the number of capillaries increases. Capillaries bring in lots of oxygen and glucose and carry away lactic acid. In this way, the muscle is able to perform for longer before tiring.

Muscle and Steroids

If you want to build stronger, bulkier, more powerful muscles, you should eat a balanced diet containing sufficient protein — because muscle is mostly made of protein — and you should exercise sensibly and regularly. You can adjust the amount of exercise and the kind of exercise to achieve the results you desire. But some athletes are so determined to build their muscles that they resort to using "anabolic steroids" to promote muscle growth and improve their performance. Use of these medications is *very dangerous* and has resulted in athletes being disqualified from the sports in which they worked so hard to excel.

Anabolic steroids are synthetic male hormones taken to enhance muscle growth and performance. To see why that would work, you need to know that hormones help regulate muscle growth. Have you ever wondered why men are able to build bulkier muscles than women? It's because men have more of the natural hormones (like testosterone) that promote muscle bulk.

Well, anabolic steroids are drugs that have effects similar to the natural male hormones. They cause the

muscle to make more of the protein molecules that fill muscle fibers. However, enhanced muscle mass and strength come at a terrible price. Anabolic steroids damage the liver, cause tumors, increase the risk of heart disease and high blood pressure, decrease the ability of the body to fight infection, trigger long bones to stop growing prematurely, cause psychological disturbances, and upset the proper balance of cholesterol. You should never use anabolic steroids. Build your muscles the safe and sensible way with a well-designed exercise program and good nutrition. Anabolic steroids are a shortcut and a cheat that can ruin your health, cut you out of the sports you wish to play, and even cut your life short.

If you were more interested in increasing the size and strength of muscle tissue, then you would want to begin resistance exercise, such as weight lifting. This type of exercise puts the muscle under more stress, but for shorter periods of time. The goal here is increasing strength rather than endurance.

Resistance exercise helps increase the size of muscle, but not by increasing the number of muscle fibers. Rather, the individual muscle fibers increase in size. The usual pattern here is short periods of intense exercise, focusing on individual muscles or sets of muscles. Then a break is taken, either by taking a day off or by engaging in a less strenuous workout. This allows the muscle to recover, providing time for the fibers to produce more of the proteins they need to contract.

Muscle Tone

Have you ever heard the term *muscle tone*? This refers to the fact that there is some tension in a muscle even when it is not being actively contracted.

Well, if there is tension in a muscle, doesn't there have to be some contraction of muscle fibers? The answer is yes, of course. But wait a minute, it was noted earlier that a muscle fiber was either relaxed or contracted (remember the all-or-none law). So how could muscle tension be there without muscle movement? The answer is simple.

Muscle tone is generated by stimulation of some select muscle fibers, not the entire muscle. There are multiple nerve fibers connecting to muscle. Alternatively, different nerve fibers stimulate different muscle fibers to contract, but in this case, not the entire muscle itself. Thus, the all-or-none law is not violated!

This mild, intermittent stimulation is helpful in keeping muscle ready to respond promptly to move intense nerve impulses.

Ever Pulled a Muscle?

Have you ever pulled a muscle? A "pulled muscle" is also called a "muscle strain." Muscle pulls often happen with sudden exertion or during athletic activity. A pulled muscle has some tears in the muscle or in the tendon that attaches it to the bone. The tears are usually small but are very uncomfortable due to the irritation of the nerve endings in the region and damage to small blood vessels with bruising inside the muscle. Swelling, bruising, weakness in the muscle, pain in the muscle and in the joint it moves during movement, and pain at rest are typical of a pulled muscle. An ice pack can help decrease the symptoms. (Be sure to avoid putting an ice pack directly on your skin. Twenty minutes of ice every hour is a good rule of thumb.) Elevating the muscle can also decrease swelling. So can an elastic bandage, but don't wrap it tightly. Rest the pulled muscle in its gently stretched position and give it time to heal before resuming the activity that injured it.

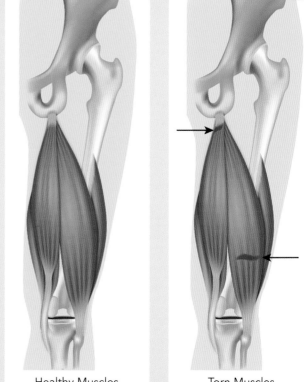

Healthy Muscles   Torn Muscles

Muscles Get Weak Too

It has been stressed over and over that to keep muscle healthy, it must be used and exercised. Unfortunately, in life there are many circumstances where muscles can go unused.

Have you ever known someone who broke an arm? The arm probably had to stay in a cast for several weeks. Do you remember what their arm looked like after the cast was taken off? The muscles were likely much smaller in the arm that was broken. Why? It's because those muscles had not been used regularly for those weeks. This is called *muscle atrophy*. The good thing is that the injured arm will soon return to normal as the arm begins to be used once again. Again, remember the phrase "use it or lose it!"

Another example is a person with a long illness that keeps them in bed for several weeks. They get progressively weaker because their muscles are not being used. Often, after an extended illness, patients will need weeks of special exercise therapy with good nutrition to help them get their strength back — to literally rebuild the protein molecules inside their muscle fibers. Remember, muscles like to be used!

Rigor Mortis

So Simple Yet So Complex — Designed by the Master

Have you ever heard that the body becomes stiff after death? This is called *rigor mortis*. Rigor mortis occurs because the muscles all over the body contract and are unable to relax. Does it seem strange that muscles would contract after death?

Ordinarily, muscles contract because calcium flows out of the sarcoplasmic reticulum and triggers actin and myosin myofilaments to form cross-bridges. Do you remember why a muscle relaxes? Muscles relax when energy from ATP is used to pump calcium away from the myofilaments and back into the sarcoplasmic reticulum. Then the cross-bridges disengage.

After death, cells cannot make ATP and soon run out of energy. Calcium ions leak out of the sarcoplasmic reticulum and trigger cross-bridges to form in muscle cells all over the body. This begins about 3 hours after death. With no more ATP being made, the calcium never gets pumped away, and the contractions stiffen the entire body. The stiffness reaches a maximum around 12 hours after death. About 36–72 hours after death, the body relaxes again because actin and myosin molecules begin to disintegrate.

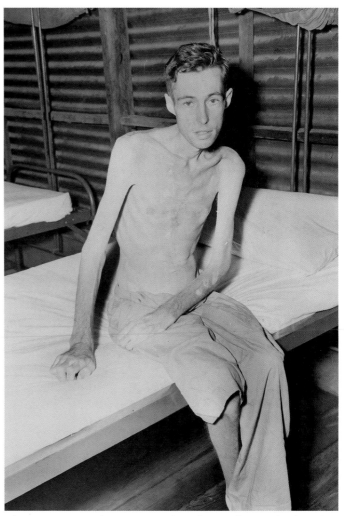

This ex-prisoner of war, Corporal Noel Havenborg (9/21/1945 in Luzon, Philippines), has suffered severe muscle loss as a result of starvation. After depleting its stored fats, the body begins to use the proteins in its muscles for fuel. Muscles may atrophy as a result of malnutrition, physical inactivity, aging, or disease.

2

MUSCLES . . .
HOW THEY MOVE ME!

It is time to take a look at a few of the major muscle groups in the body. Understandably, we will not be looking at every single muscle. After all, there are 640 skeletal muscles in your body, so trying to deal with all of them would be a bigger task than we can tackle today. We are just going to hit the high points.

So relax and enjoy our study of muscle groups.

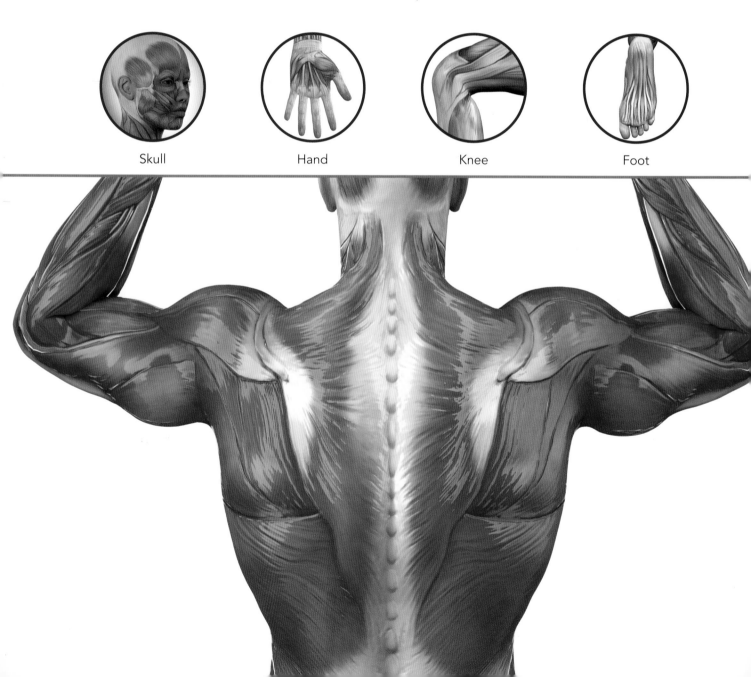

| Skull | Hand | Knee | Foot |

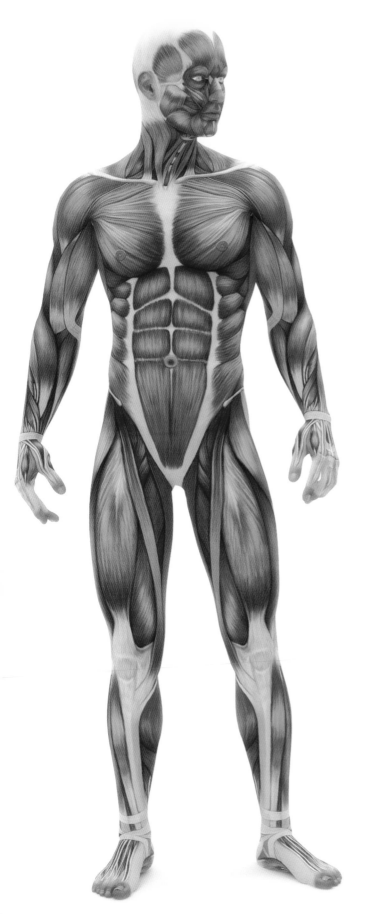

Describing Movement

Muscles move things. It is pretty much that simple. In the typical circumstance, a muscle is attached to two different bones across a joint. The muscle is connected to the bone on each end by a tendon. When the muscle contracts, the bones are pulled toward one another.

Now what do you do if you want these two bones to be farther apart again? The muscle you just used can't do it, because *muscles only pull, they don't push*. To move these bones apart, you need another muscle to do the job. You need a muscle positioned to pull in the opposite direction. Two or more muscles "oppose" one another to move bones back and forth. Muscles that work opposite each other like this are often said to be *antagonistic*. This just means that the muscles in question have opposite purposes, not that they are hostile toward one another!

It is a simple process. One muscle contracts to pull a bone in one direction while another muscle relaxes to allow the movement. To move the bone back, the first muscle relaxes while the muscle on the opposite side contracts to pull the bone in the opposite direction.

Whole Body View

Take a quick look at an overview of the major muscles of the body. I'm sure you will see many muscle names you already recognize. Perhaps you have heard of the pectoralis muscle or the gluteus maximus. Spend some time looking over the major muscle groups. Then we will explore some of these in more detail!

Naming Muscles

As we mentioned, there are over 600 muscles in the human body. At first glance, it may seem an impossible task to remember their names. But it is easier than you might think. Muscle names often *describe* the muscle in some way! Some muscles are named by their location. Some muscles are named for their shape. Some muscles are named to reflect their size. For example, the *intercostal* muscles are located between the ribs. (*Costal* means "rib," and *inter* means "between."). The *orbicularis oculi* muscle surrounds the eye. (*Oculi* means "eye," and *orbicularis* sounds a little like the word "orbit," doesn't it?) The *gluteus maximus* and the *gluteus minimus* are two of the muscles in the buttock. Can you guess which one is larger? See how easy this can be! The *trapezius* muscle in the upper back is shaped like a trapezoid. Clever, huh? Pay close attention and see if you can find other examples as we examine the major muscle groups. How muscles are named can tell you a lot about them!

The Upper Limb

If you examine the shoulder, you will see most prominently a round muscle over the cap of the shoulder. This is called the deltoid muscle. The deltoid helps rotate the arm. It also *abducts* the arm. That is, it raises the arm out to our side, *away* from the body. (Remember, *abduction* is movement away from the center of the body, and *adduction* is movement *toward* the middle of the body. If you've ever studied Latin, you'll probably recognize that *ab* means "away from" and *ad* means "toward.")

There are four muscles that hold the humerus in the shoulder joint, keeping your arm in its socket. Their names are the *supraspinatus*, the *infraspinatus*, the *teres minor*, and the *subscapularis*. These muscles allow the shoulder to have an incredible range of motion. Together, these four muscles are called the *rotator cuff*.

Remember the scapula? The large oddly shaped bone in your shoulder? Notice that the scapula has a "spine" protruding from its back side. The *supra*-spinatus muscle attaches *above* this spine, and it is named accordingly. "Supra" means "above." Likewise, the *infra*-spinatus attaches "below" the spine. Because of the way they attach to the humerus, they pull in slightly different directions. The *supraspinatus* moves the humerus up and away from the body. The *infraspinatus* and the *teres minor* externally rotate the humerus. The *subscapularis* muscle, which is attached to a depression on the lower part of the scapula ("sub" means "under"),

TAKING A CLOSER LOOK
The Chest and Shoulders

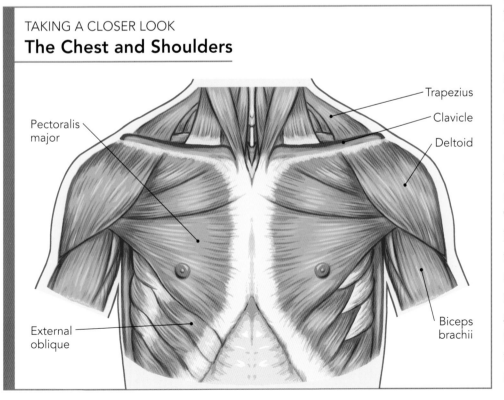

Trapezius
Clavicle
Deltoid
Pectoralis major
Biceps brachii
External oblique

TAKING A CLOSER LOOK
Rotator Cuff Muscles

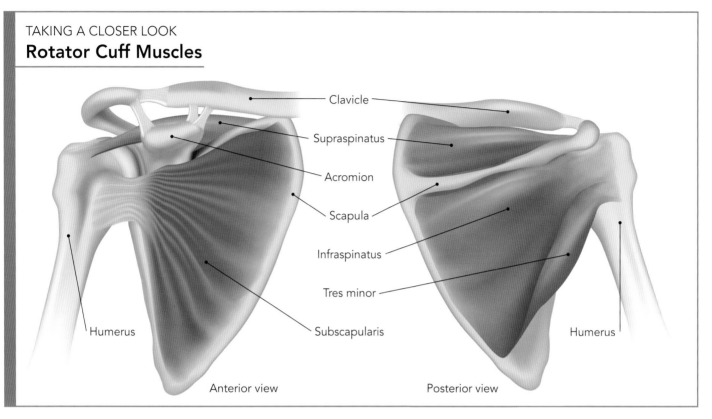

Clavicle

Supraspinatus

Acromion

Scapula

Infraspinatus

Tres minor

Humerus

Subscapularis

Humerus

Anterior view

Posterior view

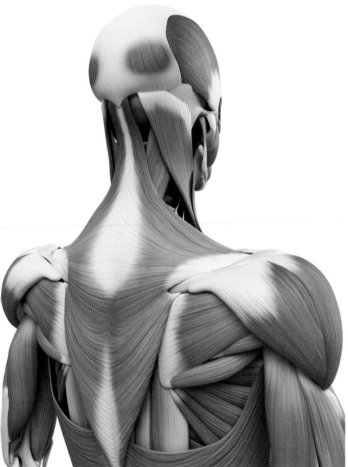

internally rotates the humerus. Thus, each muscle, because it is attached to a particular place on the scapula and on the humerus, tugs the arm from a different angle. When they work together, an infinite number of motions are possible.

The last muscle that we will mention here is called the *trapezius*. It is the triangular-shaped muscle in the upper back. It helps connect the pectoral girdle to the thorax. It helps move the scapula (shoulder blade). When you shrug your shoulders, you are using the trapezius.

Two of the best-known muscles in the body are found in the upper limb. These are the biceps, or as it is officially known, the *biceps brachii* and the *triceps brachii* (or triceps, for short). These are the muscles that flex and extend the forearm. Let's take a closer look at them.

We have already seen that muscles only pull. They do not push. So in order for full movement of the body to occur, there are muscles that work opposite one another. We called these muscles *antagonistic*. The biceps and triceps are the classic example of this arrangement.

To flex the forearm, the biceps contract (they pull the forearm, bending the elbow). However, for this movement to occur when the biceps contract, the triceps must relax. Otherwise, the forearm would not move.

To extend the forearm, the triceps contract and the biceps relax. You see, they work opposite one another.

You will see other examples of this. Can you think of others? How about your knee? One group of muscles bends the knee; another extends it so that you can kick forward. Look at your fingers. They can bend and straighten. Once again, antagonistic pairs of muscles make this happen.

The muscles of the forearm can be divided primarily into two groups, the anterior flexors and the posterior extensors. The anterior flexors flex the wrist and fingers. The posterior extensors extend the wrist and fingers.

Wait a minute! Did you say fingers? Yes, fingers. You see, even though these muscles are located in the forearm, they have long tendons to control the movement of the fingers. In this way our wonderful Creator allowed us to have very fine control of our hands while at the same time having great strength in the hands. This would not be possible if the major muscles were located in the hands themselves. There are small muscles located in the hand itself. However, the big muscles needed to supply great strength would take up so much room that our hands could not function properly.

TAKING A CLOSER LOOK
Bicep and Tricep Action

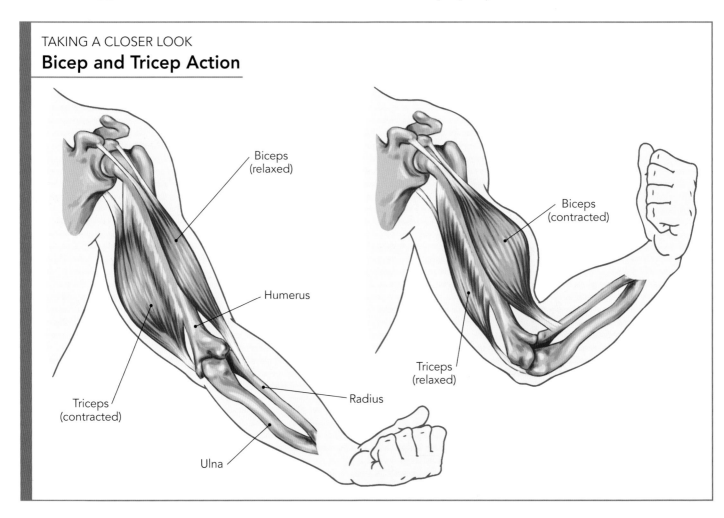

SO SIMPLE YET
Designed by the Master
SO COMPLEX

The Strongest Muscle

What is the strongest muscle in the body? The right answer is: it depends. It depends on what you mean by "strong." If by "strongest" you mean "biggest," then the *gluteus maximus* muscle is the strongest. It is the largest muscle in the body. If by "strongest" you mean "works hardest," then the heart is the strongest. The heart does the most work throughout our lives. If by "strongest" you mean which muscle generates the most force compared to its size, then the masseter—the powerful chewing muscle that closes your jaw—is generally considered the strongest.

The Chest and Abdomen

Let's learn about a few important muscles in the chest and abdomen. You may have even done exercises like sit-ups or weight lifting to make some of them stronger.

First is the *pectoralis major* muscle. Most likely you already know about this muscle. It is the primary muscle of the chest. This muscle helps flex the arm. People who work out with weights usually have very prominent pectoralis muscles!

The other important muscles in the chest are the *intercostals*. These are the muscles between the ribs. The intercostals help us breathe. We will learn more about the intercostals when we study the respiratory system.

In the abdomen, take note of the *rectus abdominis*. This long muscle on the front wall of the abdomen helps keep the pelvis stable as we walk. It also helps flex the trunk. People do sit-ups or crunches to make it stronger.

To each side of the rectus abdominis are three muscles: the *external oblique*, the *internal oblique*, and the *tranversus abdominis*. These muscle sheets are oriented in different directions. Together they support and protect the abdominal organs below them.

TAKING A CLOSER LOOK
The Chest and Abdomen

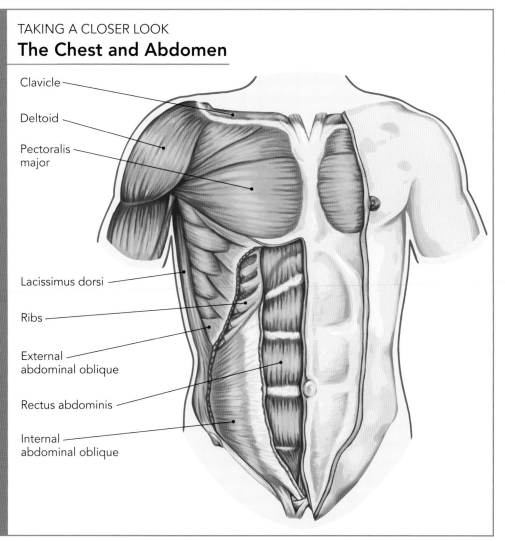

- Clavicle
- Deltoid
- Pectoralis major
- Lacissimus dorsi
- Ribs
- External abdominal oblique
- Rectus abdominis
- Internal abdominal oblique

The Lower Limb

The muscles in our legs are strong and powerful. They have to be in order to carry us around all day long.

One of the primary muscles for you to know is *rectus femoris*. It is one of four muscles in a group known as the *quadriceps*. Your "quads" extend the knee and flex the hip.

On the rear of the thigh are the *hamstring* muscles. This is a group of three muscles, the most prominent of which is called the *biceps femoris*. The hamstrings flex the knee and extend the hip. The hamstrings are the antagonists of the quadriceps.

One other muscle to mention here is the *gluteus maximus*. It forms a large part of the buttock. But your gluteus maximus does much more than give you a place to sit. This muscle extends the thigh, moving it backward.

Below the knee we find the muscles of the leg. (Remember, the upper part of the lower limb is called the thigh, and the "leg" officially refers to the lower part of the lower limb!) As with the forearm, it is easiest to consider the muscles in groups. There is the *anterior compartment* and the *posterior compartment*. Since *anterior* means "in the front" and *posterior* means "in the back," you can probably guess where these muscle groups are located. That gives you a great clue to what they do.

The muscles in the *anterior compartment* pull on the toes and *dorsiflex* the foot. That is, they flex the ankle to move the foot and toes upward.

The muscles in the *posterior compartment* flex the toes and *plantar flex* the ankle. In other words, they

TAKING A CLOSER LOOK
The Lower Limb Muscles

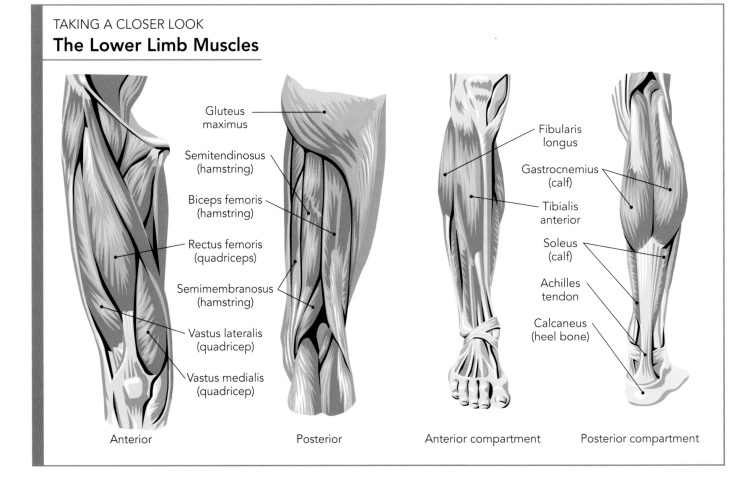

Gluteus maximus

Semitendinosus (hamstring)

Biceps femoris (hamstring)

Rectus femoris (quadriceps)

Semimembranosus (hamstring)

Vastus lateralis (quadricep)

Vastus medialis (quadricep)

Fibularis longus

Gastrocnemius (calf)

Tibialis anterior

Soleus (calf)

Achilles tendon

Calcaneus (heel bone)

Anterior   Posterior   Anterior compartment   Posterior compartment

Monkeys and Muscles

There are actually three gluteal muscles on each side of our body. (They are the gluteus maximus — the biggest one — and the gluteus medius and the gluteus minimus.) Together, they extend your thigh in a way that makes it possible for you to walk efficiently.

Apes have gluteal muscles too. If a gorilla or a chimpanzee tries to walk upright on two legs, it can manage it for a while, but must swing its thigh far out to the side. This is not an efficient way for apes to walk. God designed apes to move through the trees, but He designed people to walk. Therefore, the shape of the pelvic bones (the iliac crest, specifically), in a human, curves to allow the gluteal muscles to pull the thigh in just the right direction for us to walk.

The gluteal medius muscle tugs our thigh sideways as it extends it, allowing us to keep our balance as we walk. In an ape, the iliac crest doesn't curve but sticks out to the side; this prevents the gluteal medius muscle from pulling the thigh sideways. Therefore, an ape must sway and swing its leg to the side to keep from falling over when it tries to walk like a man.

pull your foot downward, as if you were pressing on the gas pedal of a car, and they curl your toes. In the posterior compartment you will find the *gastrocnemius* muscle and the *soleus* muscle. These are called "calf" muscles and they attach to the *calcaneus* (heel bone) via the *Achilles tendon*. The Achilles tendon is the strongest tendon in the body, and it is named after a character in a Greek myth who supposedly was defeated in battle when that tendon was cut.

As with the hand, the powerful movements of the foot and toes are controlled primarily by muscles in the leg.

The Head and Face

There is a wide array of muscles in the face. Many of these muscles anchor not to bone but to skin. Movement of these facial muscles is responsible for the amazing variety of facial expressions that human beings can make. Of course, muscles in the head and face also make chewing our food possible!

The *orbicularis oculi* muscle encircles each eye. This ring of muscle is an example of a *sphincter*. With this sphincter you can close your eyes. Surrounding the eyes and being embedded in the eyelids, it helps us blink, wink, and squint.

The main muscle across our forehead is the *occipitofrontalis*. This muscle elevates the eyebrows. If you've ever seen someone raising their eyebrows with a surprised look on their face, the occipitofrontalis was involved.

There are several muscles that move the lips and cheeks. These muscles help us eat, smile, and speak.

The *orbicularis oris* is the muscle that surrounds the mouth. This is another ring-shaped sphincter muscle. (Did you notice that the sphincters around the eyes and the mouth both have *orbicularis* in their names? Doesn't that sound like "orbit," or circling something?) Just as the orbicularis oculi closes your eyes, so the orbicularis oris helps you close your mouth. It helps control movement of the lips. This is the muscle you need to pucker up and kiss!

The *mentalis* muscle on the front of the lower jaw helps wrinkle the chin.

The *buccinator* compresses the cheek and helps keep food in place as we chew. It is involved with sucking movements, so nursing infants use the buccinators quite a bit!

Farther below you find a large, flat muscle that extends from the neck to the chin. This is the *platysma*. This muscle tenses the skin of the neck and pulls the corners of the mouth down. When you frown or grimace, you are using your platysma muscle.

SO SIMPLE YET SO COMPLEX
Designed by the Master

The Muscle with the Longest Name

You have over 40 facial muscles. Some help you chew, close your eyes, and do other critically important things. But some facial muscles mainly create facial expressions: smiles and frowns, wrinkled noses and pursed lips, wrinkled forehead and raised eyebrows. You even have a muscle to flare your nostril while lifting the corner of your upper lip! It is nicknamed the "Elvis Muscle" because the famous singer was often photographed with that expression. That muscle has the longest name in the medical dictionary: the *levator labii superioris alaeque nasi*, which is Latin for "lifter of the upper lip and the wing of the nose."

TAKING A CLOSER LOOK
Head and Facial Muscles

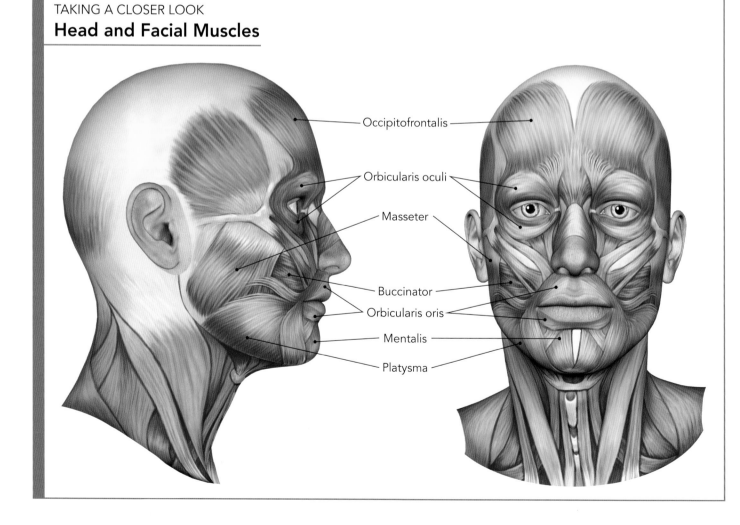

Occipitofrontalis

Orbicularis oculi

Masseter

Buccinator

Orbicularis oris

Mentalis

Platysma

Not the End, Just the Beginning

Wow! We sure have covered lots of ground.

We have studied cells and tissues, organs and organ systems. We have seen how bones and muscles work. The skeleton and muscle groups have been examined.

Throughout our journey we have stopped to give praise to our wonderful Creator. Only He, in His infinite wisdom, could have designed such a marvelous and amazing thing as the human body.

Even though we are at the end of this study there is so much more to come! This is only the beginning of our exploration of the wonders of the human body.

GLOSSARY

Abduction — movement away from the midline of the body (For example, you abduct your thigh if you kick a ball with the side of your foot while standing.)

Acetabulum — the cup-like depression in the pelvic girdle in which the rounded head of the femur moves; the hip socket

Acromegaly — a disorder in which the pituitary gland of an adult produces an excess of growth hormone (GH). This can result in physical abnormalities such as swelling of the hands and feet, enlargement of brow ridges and protrusion of the forehead, among other changes. Excessive growth hormone in a child would produce giantism, not acromegaly.

Actin — one of two myofilament types involved in muscle contraction. The thin myofilaments are actin.

Adduction — movement toward the midline of the body (For example, you adduct both of your thighs if you squeeze them together.)

ADP (adenosine diphosphate) — one of the molecules involved in energy production in a cell. When ATP (adenosine triphosphate) loses a phosphate group, energy is released and ADP is produced. The addition of a phosphate group to ADP again produces ATP (like "charging a battery").

Aerobic respiration — an oxygen-requiring series of reactions by which a cell produces energy

All-or-none law — the principle that in a given muscle fiber either all the sarcomeres contract or none of them do.

Amino acid — molecules that are the building blocks of proteins. There are 20 different amino acids used to make proteins in the human body.

Anaerobic respiration — a series of reactions by which a cell produces energy without using oxygen

Anaphase — the shortest phase of mitosis. During anaphase daughter chromosomes are pulled apart and move to opposite sides of the cell.

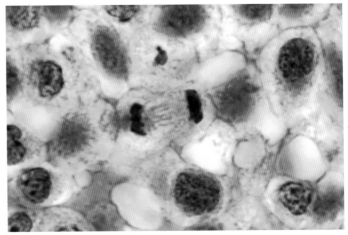

Mitosis (anaphase-telophase) in the granulosa layer of an ovarian secondary follicle

Anatomical position — standing with the palms facing forward. This position serves as a reference for describing the orientation of the body's parts. There are other positions with names too. For instance, prone means lying face down, and supine means lying face up. (With reference to the anatomical position, please see anterior, distal, inferior, lateral, medial, posterior, pronate, proximal, superior, and supinate.)

Anatomy — the study of the body's parts and how they are put together

Anterior — the front of the body (For example, the nose is on the anterior part of the head.)

Appendicular skeleton — the portion of the skeleton consisting of the upper and lower limbs as well as the bones that connect them to the axial skeleton

Arch of foot — either of several arch-shaped curves in the sole of the foot that help the foot bear the body's weight most efficiently and adjust to the changes needed to walk most efficiently; arches are formed by the relative positions of the foot and ankle bones, and they are held in place by many tendons and ligaments.

Arthritis — a joint disorder that involves inflammation of one or more joints

Arthroscopy — a surgical procedure in which a telescope-like instrument is used to look inside a joint and even to introduce long-handled precision instruments to repair tears in the soft tissues

ATP (adenosine triphosphate) — one of the molecules that stores readily available energy in the cell. When a phosphate group is added to ADP (adenosine diphosphate), ATP is produced. When a phosphate group is released from ATP, ADP is produced and energy is released (like "discharging a battery")

Axial skeleton — the portion of the skeleton consisting of the skull, vertebral column, and the ribs

Bipedal — walking upright on two legs

Calcitonin — a hormone produced by the thyroid gland. It decreases the activity of osteoclasts and reduces the amount of calcium released into the blood.

Callus — repair tissue that forms at the site of a bone fracture

Cancellous bone — another term for spongy bone

Cardiac muscle — the muscle of the heart

Cell — the most basic structural and functional unit of a living organism, such as the human body. A cell generally consists of three parts: the nucleus, the cell membrane, and the cytoplasm.

Cell membrane — the cell's wrapper. The cell membrane separates everything outside the cell from everything inside the cell, and it regulates what can and cannot go across. It consists of two layers of molecules called phospholipids. It is therefore called a phospholipid bilayer, and many important molecules are embedded in this "phospholipid sandwich."

Central canal — a channel in an osteon containing blood vessels and nerves. It is sometimes called a Haversian canal.

Centrioles — a pair of L-shaped cellular organelles involved in organizing microtubules to guide chromosomal movements during mitosis.

Chondrocyte — a mature cartilage cell

Chromatid — one copy of a duplicated chromosome

Chromosome — tightly packed portions of DNA found in the nucleus of cells. Chromosomes are generally only visible during cell division.

Collagen — the primary structural protein of connective tissue

Compact bone — the dense outer layer of most bones

Compound fracture — fracture in which the broken bone protrudes through the skin

Connective tissue — tissue that helps provide a framework for the body

Cristae — a fold in the inner membrane of a mitochondrion

Cytoplasm — the fluid inside a cell plus all of the organelles, except for the nucleus

Cytoskeleton — the network of microtubules and microfilaments inside a cell

Cytosol — the fluid portion of the cytoplasm

Diaphysis — the shaft or midsection of a long bone

Distal — located farther from the center of the body than something else (For example, the hand is distal to the elbow.)

DNA (deoxyribonucleic acid) — a molecule that contains all the genetic information that is needed for the development and function of a living organism, such as the human body

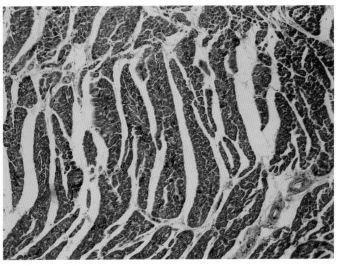

Cardiac muscle

DNA polymerase — an enzyme that assembles DNA by linking nucleotides together

Double-helix — the structure formed by DNA. It looks like a twisted ladder.

Endocytosis — a process of bringing material—usually large molecules or other things too large to be simply transported across the cell membrane—into a cell. The cell membrane folds itself around the needed material and then pinches off, forming a new vesicle inside the cell.

Epiphyseal plate — the growth plate in a bone

Epiphysis — the rounded end (joint end) of a long bone

Epithelial tissue — the tissue that lines body cavities or covers surfaces

Erythrocyte — a mature red blood cell

Evolution — the belief that all life, including the human body, developed on its own as a result of chemical reactions over million of years

Exocytosis — a process of releasing material from inside the cell. A vesicle inside the cell merges with the cell membrane, releasing cellular products into the extracellular fluid.

Extension — movement that increases the angle between body parts (For example, you extend your elbow to straighten your arm.)

Extracellular fluid — the fluid outside a cell

Fibroblast — a cell that makes collagen and the extracellular matrix.

Flexion — movement that decreases the angle between body parts (For example, you flex your elbow when you bend your arm.)

Foramen magnum — the large opening in the bottom of the skull through which the brainstem continues into the spinal cord

Fracture — a broken bone

Gene — a segment of DNA that codes for a specific protein

Genome — the complete set of genetic material of an organism. The human genome contains all the information needed to build the human body. The human genome has over 3 billion DNA base pairs.

Gigantism — a condition resulting from excessive production of growth hormone (GH) during childhood, while bones are still growing in length. Also called giantism, it can result in persons reaching excessive heights, often well over 7 feet.

Glandular epithelium — specialized form of epithelial tissue that forms the body's many glands

Golgi apparatus — an organelle responsible for the packaging and transport of many substances in a cell

Gout — a form of arthritis due to excessive amounts of uric acid in the joint capsule

Ground substance — the material that fills the space between cells in connective tissue. Also called matrix.

Growth hormone (GH) — one of the hormones secreted by the pituitary gland. Among other things, GH helps regulate bone growth.

Hematoma — a mass of clotted blood; a bruise

Hematopoesis — the process of producing new blood cells

Homeostasis — maintaining various processes and conditions within appropriate limits. For example,

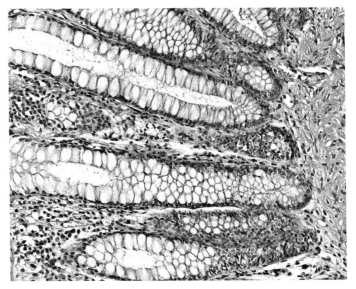

Glandular tissue at 20x Magnification

blood sugar, body temperature, and blood pressure need to be neither too high nor too low. Many homeostatic mechanisms maintain equilibrium among the body's systems.

Hydrophilic — attracted to water (literally meaning "water-loving")

Hydrophobic — something that avoids water, like oil; (literally "water-fearing")

Inferior — below (For example, the inferior vena cava is a large vein that brings blood from the lower part of the body back to the heart.)

Insulin — a hormone produced by the pancreas that helps regulate the amount of sugar in the blood

Interphase — the time in the cell cycle not directly involved with duplicating the cell

Intracellular fluid — fluid inside a cell; the cell's organelles and many important molecules are found in the intracellular fluid

Keratin — a structural protein found in hair and nails

Lacunae — spaces in compact bone where osteocytes are found

Lamellae — the rings of extracellular matrix found in compact bone

Lateral — to the side (For example, in the anatomical position, the radius is lateral to the ulna. Now you see the importance of the anatomical position. This would not be true in some other positions!)

Ligament — dense connective tissue that binds bone to bone

Lipid — an organic molecule that does not dissolve in water (hydrophobic). Fats are the most common type of lipids.

Lysosome — intracellular vesicle containing enzymes that can digest many kinds of molecules and debris

Matrix — the material that fills the space between cells in connective tissue. Also called ground substance.

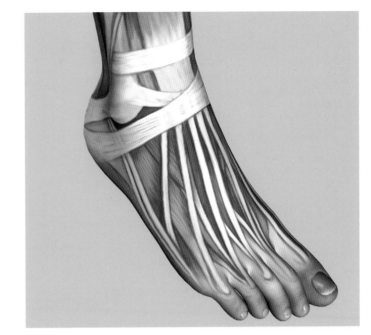
Ligaments and tendons of the ankle and foot

Medial — toward the middle (For example, in the anatomical position, the big toe is medial to the little toe.)

Messenger RNA (mRNA) — a type of RNA that is made during protein production. When a section of DNA is read (decoded), messenger RNA is produced. The mRNA then attaches to a ribosome where the information is read by molecules of transfer RNA (tRNA), and a protein is produced.

Metaphase — second phase of mitosis when the chromosomes reach the center of the cell

Mitochondria — organelles inside a cell that generate and store energy

Mitochondrial DNA — the DNA of a mitochondrion. Mitochondrial DNA is inherited only from the mother.

Mitosis — the part of the cell cycle involved with dividing a cell into two daughter cells

Mitotic spindle — a structure inside a cell composed of microtubules. This array of microtubules helps guide the cell's chromosomes during cell division.

Muscle atrophy — loss of muscle mass due to disease or disuse

Muscle fiber — muscle cell

Myofibril — rod-like structure made of myofilaments extending through the length of a muscle fiber.

Myofilament — actin or myosin

Myosin — one of two myofilament types involved in muscle contraction. The thick myofilaments are myosin.

Muscle tissue — tissue responsible for movement

Nervous tissue — tissue that is the primary component of the nervous system. The nervous system regulates and controls bodily functions.

Neurons — nerve cells

Nuclear membrane — the membrane the surrounds the nucleus of the cell

Nucleotides — the molecules that are the building blocks of DNA and RNA. The nucleotides adenine, cytosine, guanine, and thymine are found in DNA. The nucleotides adenine, cytosine, guanine, and uracil are found in RNA.

Nucleus — the control center of the cell. The nucleus contains DNA.

Organ — a group of tissue that has a particular function

Organelle — a structure within a cell that has a specific function

Osteoarthritis — a form of arthritis caused by deterioration of the joint cartilage

Osteoblast — a cell that builds new bone

Osteoclast — a cell that breaks down bone

Osteocyte — a mature bone cell

Osteon — the basic unit of compact bone

Osteoporosis — a bone disease that is characterized by a loss of bone mass

Periosteum — the membrane that cover the outer portion of bone

Phospholipid — the primary component of cell membranes. It is composed of a hydrophilic head and two hydrophobic tails.

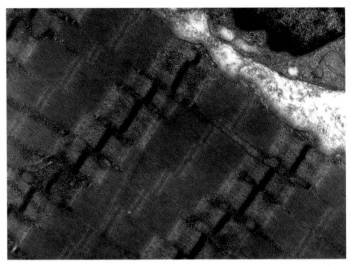

Transmission electron microscope image of a thin longitudinal section cut through an area of human skeletal muscle tissue. Image shows several myofibrils, each with distinct banding pattern of individual sarcomeres.

Phospholipid bilayer — a term to describe the plasma membrane because it is composed of two layers of phospholipids

Physiology — the study of how the parts of the body function

Plasma membrane — another name for the cell membrane

Posterior — the back side of the body (For example, the vertebral bones are on the posterior part of the torso.)

Pronate — to turn the hand (or the arm) so that the palm faces backward or downward; (also, to turn the foot so that the weight rests on the medial part)

Prophase — first phase of mitosis when the DNA condenses into chromosomes and centrioles separate by moving along newly formed microtubules

Protein — an organic compound made up of amino acids

Proximal — located nearer to the center of the body than something else (For example, the knee is proximal to the foot.)

PTH (parathyroid hormone) — a hormone secreted by the parathyroid glands. PTH stimulates osteoclasts to break down bone, thus increasing the amount of calcium in the blood.

Rheumatoid arthritis — a form of arthritis due to the body's immune system attacking joint structures

Ribosome — intracellular organelle where proteins are made

Rickets — a bone disease in children caused by Vitamin D deficiency

Rigor mortis — stiffening of the body after death

RNA (ribonucleic acid) — single-stranded molecule similar to DNA; it is involved in executing the instructions for protein synthesis found in DNA. See transfer RNA and messenger RNA.

Rotation — movement around an axis, like turning your head from side to side.

Rough endoplasmic reticulum — series of tubes and membranes connected to the nuclear membrane. Rough endoplasmic reticulum is covered with ribosomes and is involved with protein production.

Sarcomere — the simplest contractile unit of a muscle cell; each muscle cell (fiber) contains many sarcomeres.

Sesamoid bone — a bone embedded in a tendon or a muscle; the patella (kneecap) is the largest one.

Skeletal muscle — striated muscle that is attached to the bone of the skeleton

Smooth endoplasmic reticulum — a series of tubes and membranes connected to the nuclear membrane. Smooth endoplasmic reticulum is not covered with ribosomes. It is involved with the production of fats and certain hormones.

Smooth muscle — non-striated muscle found in the wall of most hollow organs of the body

Spongy bone — a type of bone that is less dense that compact bone. It is found primarily at the end of soft long bones.

Sprain — a tear or partial tear in the ligaments in the joint

Striated muscle — muscle tissue in which the orderly repeating arrangement of sarcomeres make it look striped. Skeletal muscle is striated; smooth muscle is not.

Superior — above (For example, the superior vena cava is a large vein that brings blood from the head, neck, and arms—the upper parts of the body—back to the heart.)

Supinate — to turn the hand (or the arm) so that the palm faces forward or upward (also, to turn the foot so that the weight rests on the lateral part)

Synovial fluid — lubricating fluid produced by the synovial membrane inside joints that move

Telophase — the last phase of mitosis in which the nuclear membranes re-form and the cell completes its division into two cells

Tissue — a group of cells that perform similar or related functions. There are four basis tissue types: epithelial, muscle, connective, and nervous.

Trabeculae — the functional units of spongy bone

Transfer RNA (tRNA) — a form of RNA that is responsible for transporting amino acids during protein production

Vesicle — an organelle inside the cell consisting of fluid enclosed in a lipid bilayer (similar to the plasma membrane)

Vitamin D — a molecule that aids the absorption of calcium, phosphate, and iron from the food we eat

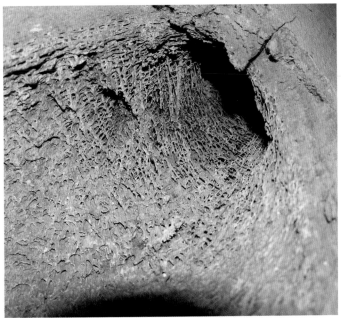

Inside of a bone showing the trabecular structure

INDEX

Photo Credits

T=Top, M=Middle, B=Bottom, L=Left, R=Right
All photos and illustrations Shutterstock.com unless noted.

iStock.com: Page 67 T

NASA: Page 53

Pubic Domain: Page 51 B (all) , Page 106

Science Photo Library: Page 20 BL, Page 22, Page 28 B, Page 46, Page 49, Page 86, Page 99

Wikimedia Commons: Images from Wikimedia Commons are used under the CC-BY-3.0 (or previous) license, CC-BY-CA 3.0, or GNU Free documentation License Version, 1.2
Page 12 T (Itayba)
Page 15 B (Blausen.com staff)
Page 19 (Nephron)
Page 21 T (Bolzer et al)
Page 44 Short Bones (CC-BY-SA 2.1 JP)
Page 63 BL (Rice University)
Page 69 (Patricia Curcio)
Page 82 B, Page 103 (Andrea Mazza)
Page 83 BL (Ganimedes)
Page 83 T, M (Rollroboter)
Page 107 B (Daniel Ullrich)

DR. TOMMY MITCHELL

Dr. Tommy Mitchell graduated with a BA with highest honors from the University of Tennessee-Knoxville in 1980 with a major in cell biology. For his superior scholarship during his undergraduate study, he was elected to Phi Beta Kappa Society (the oldest and one of the most respected honor societies in America). He subsequently attended Vanderbilt University School of Medicine, where he received his medical degree in 1984.

Dr. Mitchell completed his residency at Vanderbilt University Affiliated Hospitals in 1987. He is Board Certified in Internal Medicine. In 1991, he was elected a Fellow of the American College of Physicians (F.A.C.P.). Tommy had a thriving medical practice in his hometown of Gallatin, Tennessee for 20 years, but, in late 2006, he withdrew from medical practice to join Answers in Genesis where he presently serves as a full time speaker, writer, and researcher.

As a scientist, physician, and father, Dr. Mitchell has a burden to provide solid answers from the Bible to equip people to stand in the face of personal tragedy and popular evolutionary misinformation. Using communication skills developed over many years of medical practice, he is able to connect with people at all educational levels and unveil the truth that can change their lives.

Dr. Mitchell has been married to his wife Elizabeth (herself a retired obstetrician) for over 30 years, and they have three daughters. His hobbies include Martin guitars, anything to do with Bill Monroe (the famous bluegrass musician), and Apple computers. He does also admit to spending an excessive amount of time playing cribbage with Ken Ham.